Surrendering to Joy

Surrendering to Joy

My Year of Love, Letting Go and Forgiveness

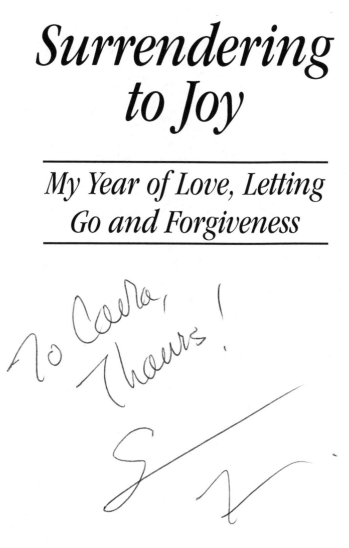

To Carla,
Thanks!

SUZANNE FALTER

Surrendering to Joy:
A Year of Love, Letting Go and Forgiveness
Copyright © 2013 by Suzanne Falter LLC

Published by: Love & Happiness Publishing (L&H)
P O Box 470
Corte Madera CA 94976

Designed by Maureen Cutajar, Go Published

Cover by Magical Marketing

Printed by CreateSpace

ISBN: 978-0-9911248-0-0

First Printing, November 2013
Printed in the United States of America

*Dedicated
to the memory of
Teal*

Contents

Introduction

THIS IS A story of letting go. Dancing through a dark tunnel, fumbling along from one signpost to the next, and believing for no good reason that at any moment an unexpected light will shine.

Of course the light was always there from the beginning, shining quite beautifully. I'd simply forgotten where to look for it.

And so I found myself with nothing to call my own in my 53rd year. That was the year I lost everything: my career, my home, the relationship I had been pinning my hopes on, my mother, and my marriage of 23 years.

And then I lost Teal.

This book is my tribute to her. It took the sudden death of my beautiful, life-loving, jubilant 22-year-old daughter for me to truly dissolve and be reborn. And to find my way back to a state of grace, and a deep and abiding joy.

Knowing Teal, that is just the way she would have wanted it; she always had a better idea of how her mother should do things.

It was only after her death that I realized she was exactly right.

The cause of Teal's death remains unknown. A housemate found her collapsed in an empty bathtub after a cardiac arrest.

EMTs managed to restore her heartbeat, but she never regained consciousness and was taken off life support six days later. Teal was an epileptic, but doctors agree a seizure was probably not the cause of her death.

Researchers estimate one in one thousand epileptics pass away from mysterious sudden deaths each year. But I believe Teal died because she was meant to become a healer from the afterlife.

Several months before her death, Teal called me and said, "In six months something really big is going to happen that will give me my healing gift." She had received this information in a meditation.

A few days after her cardiac arrest, I began to feel Teal's presence around me, talking to me and sending me this beautiful, shimmering, etheric love.

Not long after that, driven by a sense of love and peace, I began to write these essays. Each one appeared on Facebook on the date indicated, where they chronicled my slow crawl back to acceptance – and a deep forgiveness of others, but mostly myself.

It was as if Teal was sitting with me as I wrote each essay, thoughtfully guiding my choice of words with love and care.

You may wish to sit down and read the collection in sizable chunks. Or you may find you enjoy reading the essays one at a time, like a daily reader. Or you may prefer to flip here and there, browsing and reading as you go. It all works.

Each of these essays has a healing heart, offered with my wish for your own love and happiness. That is what writing these essays has done for me.

In her lifetime, Teal wanted that love and healing for all of us more than anything. And so this is our gift to you.

An Extraordinary Gift For Us All

☙ August 22, 2012. Written the day after Teal died.

HERE'S TO OUR beautiful Teal, one of the most vibrant, free-spirited souls I will ever know. Teal, I was so blessed to know you in this lifetime. Your compassion, courage and plain old sense of fun were extraordinary. And to be your mother – well, that was just an amazing, amazing privilege. I am so proud of you!

Every day of our lives together I learned something about life, love and how to be a better person from Teal. (I can still hear her saying, "Mom, PLEASE don't interrupt!") Her pace was a little slower than mine, and her sensitivity toward others was absolute. She literally guided me on how to move through the world with more grace, sensitivity, and far deeper loving kindness.

What a great thing to learn from your child.

When she passed away last night, about six hours after we took her off life support, so many nurses came to us with tears in their eyes. They were so moved by Teal. Even the chief of neurology welled up as he told us what an "amazing family" we are. We felt it and continue to feel it. That has a lot to do with Teal's deep desire for peace and love as she walked through this world.

And so she speaks to me still. In fact, there is something Teal calls "the unified field of love". It is the urge we have now to come together in grief, comfort, Spirit and trying to understand. There is only one message, according to Teal. And that is Love and Happiness.

Going through Teal's end of life – from the call that she had suffered cardiac arrest and was in critical condition to her final hours and the decision to donate her organs – was the most profoundly spiritual experience I have ever had.

Friends from all over the world have shown up after hearing the news, reaching out to us with love and compassion. And the three of us – Teal's dad and her brother and I – have truly appreciated the outreach.

So I am not suffering as much as you'd think right now. Instead, I feel a profound sense of peace and even gratitude for this experience, with occasional bursts of sobbing and grief.

The ground of being now is one of love – for what else can one take from this?

You Matter More Than You Think
꧁ August 28

AS WE MOVE out of the shock of losing our daughter Teal and into the reality of living the rest of our lives without her, it feels right to look at what has unfolded around us. Healing of so many kinds has happened – incredible healing that might never have occurred if Teal had not died.

It was Teal's fondest wish to become a healer.

Throughout her life, she was truly called to love and nurture people from the bottom of her heart. People remembered it. At the Celebration Party for her life that we had in San Francisco a few days ago, we heard from an incredible array of friends – from her fellow shy girl baristas in their early twenties to the tough street guys who were brought down by Teal's smile at the gym where she boxed.

We heard from a prominent life coach in the Bay Area who went out to lunch with Teal to advise her on her career path – and ended up being coached by Teal instead. And from a young man who dated Teal and shared the sweetest story of watching the Transit of Venus with her on their last night together.

Along the way over these past few weeks, I have healed some of my own relationships in amazing ways as well. First I was joined by my former husband, Larry, and our son, Luke, the day after her cardiac arrest. Larry and I have been divorced less than a year; so this, alone, has been extraordinary.

Then I was reunited in the sweetest conversations of forgiveness and gratitude with the woman I dated and then lived with after my divorce. This came after a painful breakup four months ago, when we stopped talking to each other. Since Teal's death, I've seen healing between brothers and sisters, estranged friends, distant colleagues, and even in professional relationships that seemed mired in struggle and suffering.

Truth emerges at times like this, when we learn that it is always informed by love – not by pettiness and anger.

All of us who have been touched by Teal's death are now swimming in something called "The Unified Field of Love." I first heard about this from Teal, a few nights after her collapse as she lay unconscious in the hospital. That night I woke to find her beautiful light, lemony energy – so full of flowers of happiness and joy – shimmering all around me. And this message stood out powerfully.

Since then I have come to understand so much more.

The Unified Field of Love is an energetic connection that binds us all in its beautiful, loving embrace. It is perhaps just another name for the Oneness that so many religious and spiritual traditions impart. And it is indeed an energy field of unconditional love which, when you surrender to it and let it embrace you, cushions and comforts you and heals you like nothing else.

This is essential to the healing of the world right now.

In The Unified Field of Love, you matter greatly in your perfect You-ness. You are whole, complete and gracious, no matter how troubled, incomplete or questioning you may feel. There is nothing barren, disciplinary or severe about The Unified Field of Love.

It is shaped in a perfect divine flow by your own open-hearted embrace of what is. And it is fed by your own sense of generosity, compassion and empathy for yourself and for others.

In The Unified Field of Love, all are welcome, none is

spurned, and no one is judged. A person's quirks are simply their amusing quirks; a person's limitations are simply the growth path they have chosen. All is in balance. All is in harmony. And all is well. It is a convergence of many disparate parts brought together in a stunningly perfect design.

It is, quite simply, the experience of heaven on earth.

Wonderfully, in The Unified Field of Love, you are not your wounds, your history or your "story" – that long-told, earnestly believed saga of what happened to you. Instead, you are simply a Being and your only job is to Be. You're not required to think, strategize, control, manipulate, manage or out-think.

You are simply invited to Be – as in exist, with a heavy overlay of love and gratitude for the simple pleasure of being alive. So when you walk outside the air becomes sweeter, the sky bluer, and the leaves on a thousand trees rustle softly with the music of breezes. The worlds within and without are perfect and you are invited to sink into that place of letting go and acceptance.

Let go of all your cares and concerns for just a moment if you can. Just close your eyes and feel your perfect rightness, wherever you are at this time and in this moment. And if you can allow yourself, feel the upswell of love in your heart for the world, for those around you and for yourself.

Let yourself just experience the incredible bliss of loving deeply – and being loved – even if you think you don't have a name or a face to attach to this experience.

Yes, you do matter more than you think. You matter hugely, and your ability to dissolve into The Unified Field of Love could be your greatest contribution to this world. When you do, the world begins to spin again, just as it should.

And that can make all the difference.

Returning to Bliss

IT IS OFTEN thought that, in the best of times, we live in bliss and in the worst of times, well, life is simply hell. I'd like to argue that point.

What if even in the worst of times one can experience an unusual sort of bliss? That is what this particular moment has called forth from me as I adjust to losing Teal. I am now in the sort of transition one would usually call a tragedy or even a crisis.

Yet, in the heart of this crisis, what I am experiencing more and more is a remarkable sense of calm. I have, of course, been radically changed by this experience, as have Larry and Luke. And, yes, we are grieving – sometimes together and sometimes alone.

What is happening more and more for me, personally, is an emergence, a blinking into an entirely new light. This is a place that is beyond explanation, control, or even comprehension. It is truly a field of bliss – and it continues on and on, expanding when I allow it to fill my heart a little more every day.

So what am I so blissful about, one might ask, now that I can never see, speak to, hold or even talk to my beloved daughter again? Now that I can never listen to her on the phone, perhaps crying through her fear or frustration, or possibly excitedly reporting her latest triumph?

How in God's name can I be blissful of all things?

I can only say that this mysterious bliss transcends such small concerns. It is a state of grace that is liquid, potent and transports me instantly. I literally transcend my circumstances when I let go of my suffering.

Our logical minds want so badly to make sense of this old world. How we desperately want to navigate our way through uncertainty, imagining untold conversations and fixing our sites on certain outcomes. And, yet, there is no certainty to be had, ever, under any circumstances.

All of those hopes and projections are truly just illusions. And illusions must be dashed in order to know this extraordinary bliss.

Believe me, I did not sign up for this experience willingly – nor did I resist it unwillingly. I just went with it, from the minute I received the call from San Francisco General Hospital telling me my daughter was in critical condition. I knew I had no choice – even when neurologists told us about Teal's irreversible brain damage and explained that there was nothing more they could do. We had no choice even when we held her, dying, in the sweet, spiritual silence of her hospital room as we felt her slip away.

There are only two ways to respond to anything that troubles you in life. You can accept it, surrender and go with it or you can resist. To resist the fact that Teal would never have more than these 22 years was simply to miss the point.

She was not unfortunate to have died so young. She was extremely fortunate to have had a life at all – and certainly lucky to be born with a character so willing, so free, and so committed to joy. And we were blessed beyond measure to know her.

Teal's life truly was a brilliant and shining example of that infinite bliss – despite the panic and anxiety attacks she suffered nearly every day. And despite the fact that she was an epileptic, dependent on a cocktail of brain-altering meds that kept her seizures at bay. Still she made her way, travelling around the world with her backpack, her guitar and a cardboard sign that read, "Hello, my name is Teal. I hope you enjoy the show! With Love."

And so her death is not a tragedy but a reminder to live just a little more honestly. A little more bravely. To truly treasure the minutes you have, for real – not just with some polite politically correct lip service. But to really get in there and *embrace* your life.

That means eradicating what is not true and aligned for you – the situations, relationships, agreements and bad ideas in which you've plunged yourself. I'm not talking about next week or next year or when you have more money or time, dear friend. I'm talking about now.

Ask yourself where you have held yourself back from joy. What are you resisting that must simply be owned and, ultimately, honored?

This is where the bliss is. It is a rightness that you simply know in your body; it is You talking to you. It is nothing less than your soul informing you what must shift – right here and right now – so you can truly surrender to joy.

All that you will gain is happiness, no matter what you must stop resisting and no matter how much pain you must endure to begin letting go. This, as we all know, is the true path to peace and happiness. And now the choice is yours.

Will you surrender to the bliss that awaits you … for once and for all?

Why You Are Not Alone

I AM HERE to report that I have been changed by the death of my daughter. And I have gratitude for this change, for I believe I will emerge a better person.

What such a radical experience of the quickness of life and the finality of death does for you, basically, is put you on notice.

Now I find myself naturally living much of the time in my Higher Self through no thought or inclination of my own. It's just happening. I find I am on my best behavior, looking out for all around me as I begin to see that we are all in this short life together. Gone is the natural selfish inclination I have always stumbled through life with. This has been replaced by a new humility.

This super-caring is a natural thing. It first came to me as I sat with Teal in the hospital one afternoon during her final week. She remained unconscious, encased with tubes, wires, and thermal wrapping to keep her chilled below her normal body temperature. The medical team caring for her still operated as if she would live. Yet I knew in my heart that she would die. The ethereal version of Teal had already told me that she had decided to cross over.

There we were, alone amidst ten different quietly beeping and whirring monitors, when the peace that passes all understanding began to creep from her body into mine. She had "died" three days earlier only to regain her heartbeat after 30 lifeless minutes. Yet she was no longer really there. Teal had ascended the minute she was struck.

Now divine energy began to seep into my body like a very tranquil river of peace. My stress and worry – so much a part of that time – suddenly melted away. Pure spiritual presence was with me. I couldn't see or hear it, but I could feel an otherworldly joy and calm flow from her lifeless hand directly into mine.

Quietly, slowly, a wordless exchange began between us. It was a knowing, a knowing that life is to be trusted, all of it – the good, the bad and the desperately sad.

Suddenly, I felt more solid in my chair, more alive in the world. I could feel the extraordinary responsibility of this life that I had been given. It was not unlike the knowing that passed between us the very first morning of Teal's life as her tiny, swaddled self was laid on my chest and she calmly looked me in the eye.

In that stillness, as I sat beside her dying body, I felt like I had been released from my old way of being. All at once I knew there was no longer anything to be feared in this waking, walking life – not even the death of one so beloved as my beautiful daughter. I could simply trust the surrender I was experiencing and know that God is, indeed, always benevolent.

Later, as I walked out of her room and down the hospital corridors, I observed orderlies and nurses, the mopping custodian, intent looking doctors and weary med students, even the occasional homeless person coming and going. And I saw them all with a new empathic tenderness.

These people were my people. In fact, they are your people, too. But only if you can open up your heart and claim them. Only if you are bold enough to understand that you are not any more special than anyone else. And that all of us – strangers and friends alike – need each other.

As I walked through the hospital, I understood that every path ultimately leads to growth and expansion. And that even the path of grieving and sadness has its own beauty and majesty. There is power and magic to claim in the tears we all must cry in this short life. For here, in the saddest moments, life is claimed completely.

This is how I have been changed most dramatically by Teal's death. Believe me, this is not business as usual for me. Like everyone else on this little planet, I was born from love and will return to that love when I die. Yet in between there has been a considerable bit of struggle. I know I'm not alone here – for this is what we all seem to do.

We forget about that natural ground of being, that pure state of love and consciousness we swim in at birth. And so we get busy making our lives difficult. We make the world wrong, and ourselves along with it, until we begin to hate everything except a few primal pleasures. And we cling to them desperately.

The judgments that you may have grown up with, those you harbor against others and, most of all, against yourself, are simply illusions, as are mine. There is nothing to them, for they are simply stories – just wisps of consciousness we have created to protect ourselves. And they get bitter and brittle over time until, eventually, they turn to dust when we die.

Do not lose sight of your beautiful heart. It is your direct link to God. Here you will reclaim yourself, but only if you are willing.

Please ask yourself: Can you open up and love the rest of us? That is the only question that truly matters here and now, in the quick of life.

The Ceaseless River of Joy
 September 13

I AM BEGINNING to understand the source of the joy that has been pouring through me intermittently since Teal's death a month ago.

The Joy – and, yes, this is Joy with a capital J– is an innate Joy we are all born with. It is a sacred elixir we are gifted with when we are born. It is as precious to our being as our mother's milk. Teal understood this Joy and lived it as passionately as any person can.

No, she didn't graduate from college. Nor did she put much value in earning a good living. She got along on a tiny amount of money that she created herself. When we moved her things out of her rented room in an apartment in San Francisco, it took all of an hour. Her bed was a freebie from a friend, and she had a broken bureau she found on the street. Most of her clothing was found in some paper bags in the basement of another house she had occupied along the way – which, in typical Teal style, fit perfectly and looked great on her.

She left behind an estate of exactly eight dollars, plus an incoming paycheck that might arrive ... who knows when?

Yet Teal was as happy as a person can be. Her Joy was the contagious sort – that of a person who loves their friends, loves having fun, and feels lucky to be alive at this time and in this place. Her epilepsy and her frequent panic and anxiety attacks were on her mind, but they did not control her. She was excited to be going back to college to study again and was poised to become the San Francisco leader for her beloved women's support group, Tribal Truth.

Teal did a lot with her 22 years: martial arts, cake decorating, skydiving, teaching English in Ghana, attending the Berklee College of Music and singing the blues in Austin, Texas. She hula hooped, street busked, wrote songs, worked as an organic farmer in Europe, and solo backpacked all over the world from Denmark to Laos to Morocco. She even auditioned for Broadway shows as a child and had a role in an indie feature film when she was 15.

At the end of her life, what Teal loved the most was helping people. She raised money for Planned Parenthood and facilitated group meetings for women who wanted to live their dreams. Her deepest desire was to become a healer – a gift which she felt she could receive at any moment. And she considered herself a channeler, receiving shorty, pithy guided messages and visions on a regular basis.

And so it was that she called me up the night before her collapse, in a weird foreshadowing of the events to come.

I was busy preparing for some dinner guests, but Teal made me stop, sit down and listen to her. "The last few days have not been good," she began.

She thought she was close to having a big seizure – though it could just be a string of panic attacks, she said. She never could tell. We discussed going to the neurologist the next day, something she resisted strongly. "No, Mom. They're just going to change my drugs and I like these."

The meds for epilepsy are invasive and scary, but effective. And they are heavy duty. Over the years her side effects included compulsive eating, weight gain, short-term memory loss, trouble tracking conversations, wild mood swings, exhaustion and intense anxiety.

Teal wasn't up for any more experimentation.

The conversation shifted to how much she wanted to heal women with these same panic and anxiety attacks. "I know it's what I'm here to do," she said.

We talked about the purpose of the panic and anxiety in her life, and she began to relax. She knew that in order to heal others she would have to heal herself first – to find her way through her current experience to a place of peace.

"Thanks, Mom," she said at the end of our chat. "I feel so much better now."

Neither of us could have imagined that she would be given her stage as a healer only in her death.

We all pay attention when someone like Teal dies because we must. Not just because of the tragedy of losing someone so young, but because she lived full out. We all know that incandescent Joy of hers, for it is ours as well. Yet how often do we live it? Many of us touch it at times, but do we truly embody it?

So it is only when that irrepressible Joy is finally lost that we actually wake up. But here is the good news.

We are, first and foremost, instruments of Joy.

We are run by our desires for good reason. Not because they are meant to shame us or make life difficult, but because they can enlighten us and so we can enlighten others. These are our purest desires – not those that do us or any other harm. They are the pure gold and silver born of love and gratitude.

And this living river of desire can pour through us freely, but only when we let it. It is this desire that suggests instincts to follow and talents to pursue, friendships to begin and adventures to have. Yet most of us are afraid of such freedom; for to "unplug" and follow your desires carries with it so much uncertainty.

At such times, however, uncertainty really is to be trusted.

There isn't a neurologist or a cardiologist who can say with certainty why Teal died. She did not appear to have a seizure at the time of her death; her heart failure is truly unexplainable. So we can only conclude it happened so she could continue her path to Joy even more completely. And, in doing so, she can lead us to our own ceaseless, rushing river of Joy as well.

A few days before Teal's death, while she lay in a coma, she began appearing to friends and to her father in visions. In these visions, she was serene, happy and truly content. "Things are good on the other side," she seemed to be saying. "So relax, y'all, and go have some fun."

We're listening, Teal.

And, believe me, I am writing about this Joy of yours – and ours – as fast as I can.

Getting From Pretty Good to Great
❧ September 24

SOMETHING POWERFUL AND subtle has been happening to my view of the world since Teal died. Put simply, I no longer have any tolerance for that which is "almost" in life.

As in almost good enough. Almost the right fit. Almost true. Or almost satisfactory.

Instead, what I am left with is a burning commitment to pursuing my own personal truth in a way I have never known before. So often in life I accepted what was pretty good, figuring I could never get what was "great."

I took "pretty good" jobs in advertising, which was a "pretty good" career in that it yielded nice money and interesting travel, despite the fact I was doing something I did not believe in at all. I clung to that career for 18 years.

And though much of my marriage was truly great, the last several years were only "pretty good" because I knew my sexuality was changing. I could not bear to admit that I had gone from pretty straight to more gay than straight in midlife – and that everything would have to change, as heartbreaking as that was.

I did what we so often do; I hid from the truth. I clung to the beautiful past of my marriage, when my dear husband and I were so aligned. And so I lived in a bossy blend of sentimentality and control. I was afraid and this fear controlled everything.

What I know now after the wake-up call of Teal's death is

that our lives are extremely short. And, furthermore, we have no control over our destinies. We are only players on a stage, as Shakespeare put it. We have our exits and entrances and we play many parts, just as life would have it.

And so we become lulled to sleep by aging and the natural progression of events, so undisturbed for so many of us. We expect to grow old, spend our pensions, keep our comforting love by our sides and let our dreams and deepest impulses die a quiet, secret death.

However, we now live in a radical time of change.

And some of us are being challenged to step forth and tell those visceral truths that we may have been avoiding. We are being requested to shake up our systems and take our destiny in our own hands. We have an opportunity to wake up and surrender to the truth right before us.

A few observations about this process:

1. **We get fascinated by our own story.** And it stops us. Our story is certainly noteworthy, and full of intriguing turns and twists. But it is only what happened once to us. Today is, indeed, a different day.

2. **We have vast creative powers, far beyond what we can even fathom.** Even brain scientists humbly admit they cannot explain this. Yet how we forget. We believe we are hamstrung by circumstance, or we buy into the pathos of the moment, or we sink into our story. And so we live as little souls instead of big ones.

3. **Something about suffering seems noble.** And, yet, is it really? Why isn't fun a deeper, higher, more glorious value? For this is when we are truly illuminated by God – when we are in the heart-fired experience of Joy. That Joy can be the simply

sharing of a smile from the heart or it can be when we are creating in the "zone" and time slips away. Any and all of it counts.

4. **We forget to take glorious care of ourselves.** Why should we, if our world view is that life is hard? Our bodies are a gift from God. And in that body is a specific code that will tell you just what it needs to thrive in beauty, energy, and blissful good health.

5. **Our true work is easy.** It is what we were wired to do from birth; it feels familiar even if we know nothing about it. And to discover it, you only need to pay attention to your desires. They will navigate you to just the perfect work in which you can tap into flow and sail easily along.

You deserve a life of beauty and bliss. The real questions are: Can you stand it? Can you open your arms to yourself and receive all this Joy and the happiness that accompanies it? Can you exist in bliss? Can you give yourself exactly what you want and need?

And so it goes. The mortal coil is full of lessons for all of us at any moment. All you have to do is listen, feel and discover.

The Incredible Value of Uncertainty
❦ September 28

OH, LIFE! HOW it plays with us, pushing us here and there like a well-chewed catnip toy. That is my experience as I start to rebuild my life from a place of nothing. What I know is that my fear of the uncertain future looming on the horizon is the fear we all share.

Uncertainty sucks. But does it have to?

What I'm feeling right now as I contemplate going back to California and leaving my former home in New York is true terror. Once again I leave my ex-husband and my son, and the very place I defiantly drove a moving truck away from two years ago.

The last time I left I cried and felt vulnerable for sure. But now I am leaving as a humble, very small woman. For a new life is unfolding in the wake of losing Teal.

In short, I am waking up.

Life's unpredictability has been visited upon me in extraordinary measure because children are sacred. We rely on them as the one certain thing in an uncertain world. Our job as parent and sacred caretaker becomes our rudder in life.

When you lose a child, all of that certainty is instantly lost. And so God is taking me on his own course to places I cannot imagine. Yet this is all part of a divine plan, isn't it? How else can I hold it?

When Teal died, I was drifting. I had let go of my San Francisco apartment to move into a new place in Sausalito with my girlfriend of 14 months. Two months later she abruptly ended our relationship, telling me she wasn't in love with me – nor had she ever been. So not only had I lost my first committed relationship with a woman, I lost the home that came with it.

I had also recently let go of a successful business to create a new body of work. Exactly what that will be remains unclear.

So here I am, living out of a suitcase and moving toward some bright light in the future that is not here yet. A light that my mind, with its propensity to plan, control, organize and manage, can barely tolerate. A light that is so bright it is frightening.

What if I am consumed by it? What if it is too brilliant to touch? What if I never reach the source of the light and my path just keeps getting longer and longer?

What if my doubting mind plays with the divine plan just enough that I cannot reach this place of exaltation, of consecration, of peace?

What if I die with my potential still unlived? What if my ultimate gift is not given?

What if birthing these two amazing children is the only contribution I will really ever make to this world? Does that count? Will God be disappointed if somehow I can't fulfill the rest of my promise in this life?

What am I to do, exactly, next and next and next? Where is the sweet rhythm of the predictable in my days? Will my life ever be knowable and certain again?

Or is everything ripped raw of expectation and planning – so I, too, must be opened up?

We are nothing but heart in the end. We are just love, poured into a complex package of bargaining, wielding, measuring and managing. And our ability to return to that sweet uncomplicated love is what guides our growth.

And so uncertainty must be our teacher and our master. Its guidance is complete in its void. For when we just go with that murky flow, we really "are" nothing. Then the love just naturally comes pouring in.

Just as water must flow through a sluice, it has to. There is no stopping this natural movement toward love and happiness; it is what God has mandated for all of us. All we have to do is honor it.

No worry. No regret. No mucking around in the past. No writhing in self-pity, guilt or a thousand complicated stories.

A clear eye on the future and a firm hand on the rudder is what is indicated here. I am learning to tolerate this new path, this new emptiness.

And I am finding a certain beauty in living out of that suitcase, not knowing exactly where I will go. What I know is that my writing and speaking are guiding me, like a port in a storm. Each time I surrender to the words that want to come out, I feel sanctified.

Last night I dreamed about something extremely beautiful – what I can't even say. But Teal popped in with a hearty, "YEAH!" And I woke up knowing that, yes, the path to Joy actually *is* the plan here.

Joy as in deliciousness – like the perfect lemon tart. Or comfort – like the perfect ray of sunlight streaming into my kitchen. Or the perfect joy of singing, or making love, or swimming, or writing.

And so uncertainty has led me squarely back to the bright light of Joy. Why should I be surprised? That is how we all come into this life, isn't it?

And how, if we are paying attention, we may return.

Are You a Drama Junkie?

❦ October 6

PERHAPS THIS QUESTION caught your attention; I know it struck me when I thought of it. In truth, I have observed that so many of us, including me, ARE drama junkies.

See if you can relate: You are busy just trying to get along. You do your best to show up fully for your family or friends. You meditate when you can bash your way through to an open spot in your schedule. You honestly do your best to wade through the stuff of life to get to a little peace.

Life is hard.

But somehow you never feel fully in control; everything happens a little too fast. The wild and unexpected seems to keep showing up, derailing everything. You are used to just getting your feet under you just before all hell breaks loose again. And again. And again.

It's miserable, isn't it?

Teal's death ripped the lid off my pretentions about myself. At the time I was a "busy" entrepreneur, casting about to get a new business started and doing my best to recover from a tortured, messy breakup rife with drama.

A lot of my thoughts and my time were consumed with how injured I was. Defiantly, righteously, I was licking my wounds. I had a really good story about why others should take pity on me and give me a soft shoulder to cry on. Lo the drama!

Then the unthinkable happened and my beautiful girl died. As my mother used to put it, now I REALLY had something to cry about. But here is the truly remarkable thing: Suddenly, I no longer felt like a sad, pitiful victim.

Yes, I have done my work over the years – and my propensity for drama was certainly waning. But in this radical situation, the worst thing that can possibly happen to a mother became my salvation.

Teal's death showed me how vastly unimportant my own little stories are, and how profound, rich and abundant my life can be when shared in true service.

During the six days when Teal was on life support, my former partner stepped in to help. Quickly, we dismissed what had been months of anxiety, unfairness and hurt feelings because now only one thing mattered: Teal and her impending death.

Life was snapped up tight before us. It was no longer the loose, blowsy meandering path that demanded little of us. Instead, the Truth had arrived, its white light blazing, and we could see what small, insignificant creatures we were in its grand scheme.

All of our drama is nothing more than the mechanics of a childish mind – one that has not yet seen the vast opportunity of this life we have been given.

Did you know that you are brilliant, gifted and profound, but only if you quiet down and tune into that brilliance?

Did you know that you can solve all of the problems handed to you, but only if you accept that vast, soaring power of yours?

Did you know that you are a sensitive and supreme being who only has to claim your sweet supremacy? We are ALL born innately supreme – every last one of us. Yet we are afraid to cash in that chip in life and so we suffer.

To stop the drama, you have to surrender to your own intrinsic ability to heal yourself. And nothing starts that process faster than the admission that you are not your sad story and that you really can give yourself a break and move on.

In my own tortured breakup, I saw I was not actually the victim but the willing co-creator of the drama. I was 100 percent responsible for that big, fat learning experience, but hoping someone else would pick up my sadly broken pieces.

Instead a beautiful thing has happened. I am learning to pick up my own pieces now. Teal's death was such an extreme yank back to reality that there simply isn't any other choice.

And so I am slowly becoming a woman who can take care of herself, without needlessly obsessing over my sorry lot. And such is possible for all of us drama junkies.

If you feel the pull to drama, perhaps you can dissolve into all that love and joy. When you do, your self-care becomes deeper and more tender. It becomes less about how wounded you are and more about being of service to others. When your circumstances no longer matter that much, then you can focus gorgeously on each new gift you have to share.

And that is when we truly start to have fun.

Take a look at where life is rubbing you the wrong way right now. Is it really that critical? Or is there some way to shake loose the perception of failure, fear or impending disaster?

I promise you are infinitely capable of dissolving back into the big Joy that is your birthright. Right here and right now. All you have to do is allow it in.

Nothing will make God happier.

A Few Good Places to Look for Joy
∾ October 11

RECENTLY A FRIEND mentioned to me how hard it was for her to experience genuine Joy. She knew calm and even peace pretty well, but that deep-in-the-belly Joy had eluded her. She could not quite grasp it somehow.

Oh, how she wanted it. The desire was burning in her.

What is interesting is the paradox of the situation. For as long as you grasp and long for things, and feel the barricades of your mind drop down, and know that singular hopelessness of being human, Joy is elusive.

You cannot force genuine happiness any more than you can force a butterfly to land upon you. All you really can do is become present to what is. And then you start to melt into the very truth of what is happening here and now.

There is something beautiful in this truth. In the feeling and savoring of it, we are immediately reborn. Mind you, I'm not talking about anything more complex than feeling what is right in front of you right here and right now.

Try this for a moment: Pick a situation where you find a lot of personal resistance. And just allow yourself to feel it.

I'm thinking about the fact that I feel very vulnerable right now. This morning I got a California Driver's License, the first license I've had in 25 years that didn't have my married name on it. I'm Suzanne Falter again and this feels tender and scary to me.

It's symbolic of the fact that I am really alone now. My

daughter is gone, I am 3,000 miles from my son, and I am divorced and single. I am finding a home and carving out an entirely new life for myself. It is up to me to pull on big girl panties and make decisions for myself.

I can feel my resistance to this concept. Can I trust myself to make the right decisions? Do I have what it takes to be a truly powerful, peaceful adult?

Can't somebody do all of this for me?

Please?

My mind spins and reels with wreckage from the past, proof that I can't think my way out of a paper bag. Long mental diatribes ensue. I am toast.

Then I stop for a moment and just breathe. I feel the inevitability of growing up and my pain increases. I feel the fear come pouring into my lungs, worry creases my brow, and tension knits my shoulder blades together. How will I ever get through this? I feel like I am being compressed into a tight little iron box.

And, yet, as I continue to breathe into the pain, something opens up. The invisible shield cracks and a ray of hope slips in. By letting myself go so deeply into that feeling of despair, I give myself a chance. Ironically, something good suddenly starts to shift and stir.

Maybe growing up isn't so bad. Maybe being "just me" with my old name and the scratchings of a new life isn't so terrible after all. A sudden realization sneaks up on me: I can create this life any old way I want.

I feel relief. And so I begin to meander back to Joy.

This is what is available to all of us in each an every moment we are alive. We are creativity machines, constantly generating new cells, new life and a passel of new possibilities with each breath.

And, of course, we forget. Why should we remember? We

are too busy filling our heads with complexity to tap into this simpler, easier view of life. That simple return to Joy is always possible.

Just by breathing into what is and by letting it crack us open again and again and again, we can get there. There is no shame to this journey, dear friend. It's the human condition and we can actually hold it as the miracle it is.

We simply have to recognize that whatever is upon us is like a sheep in wolf's clothing. It is a surprise gift disguised as a worry or a problem. To unwrap it, we must simply savor that package and accept it with all we have.

This is the truest path back to inner peace. When we remove our innate resistance to what is, we can relax, once again, into the sweet embrace of God.

Somebody Somewhere Loves You

⟨𝒜⟩ October 24

ONE OF THE things that has been waking me in the night lately is an incredible feeling of aloneness. It haunts me, bringing me back to an empty desert of tears again and again.

In that desert, I believe I have lost my family. When I have these thoughts, I decide I am totally alone and so it breaks my heart.

My son and my ex-husband are carved into my heart as family always is. There is something indelible, lasting, and forever in our connection – just as there continues to be a connection with Teal.

So when I calm down and tell the truth about it, I realize that despite our circumstances, all of us, including Teal, *are* still together. We are ineluctably merged, no matter where we are or how our paths unfold.

As a mother, I have known my children's hearts better than anyone. I could feel their shyness and their tender ambitions. I've known their fears, their obstacles and their deepest desires. It's not a conscious knowing. It's more of a feeling. I just do. Somehow.

This is the terrain of a mother, the life link we are given when our children are born. In a similar way, we are always linked to the co-creator of this child, our other, our spouse. That history of lessons, decisions, projects, gains, losses, transgressions and forgiveness is huge.

Without it, who would we be? For in this way we are connected intrinsically through our personal histories. We are handed the keys to heaven in every relationship. Our ability to honor the path, and the rightness of our dynamics in each moment, is our salvation.

Of course, we can't get love "right" any more than we can control how another will move through our life. But control is not the point – genuine love and understanding is.

If we can approach each partner, friend, spouse and lover as our teacher and guide, we can experience the heaven in that relationship. Then no one has to be any way other than they are – and so both can grow together.

Then we actually have the opportunity to learn from one another. For who are they really? Do we even know? Or do we see them from behind our own fine screen of illusion, formed through all of our years of emotional ups and downs?

We are solidly parked in the "reality" of life – a place of hopelessness, despair, dissatisfaction and unrest. We believe that our lot is limited, and we let logic dictate our dreams. Yet there is a thread of magic that connects us all, inviting us deeper into the mystery of life.

When I remember this, I feel connected again to my son and my former husband. I know that energetically they are right here with me, just as Teal always is. I can transcend the restrictions of my thinking mind, and even have rich and delicious telepathic chats with them – as can we all with those we love.

Two years ago, as I left my former life, my son took off for a year as an exchange student in Taiwan. We all had a tearful goodbye at the gate at the airport, knowing we would never again be the same family again.

Yet one month later my boy visited me in a dream. He came to me, smiling, from the other side of the world, as if to say, "It's OK, mom. I'm happy and so are you. Everything is great!" Wordlessly, we felt each other deeply in our embrace.

My former husband had a similar encounter with Teal as she lay dying in the hospital. In his vision, she stood outside the hospital, dressed in a simple grey sweatshirt and jeans. She was smiling radiantly. "I'm great, Dad. And everything is going to be fine," her wordless smile told him.

And so it is. We are not alone. For whoever you are, and no matter what your circumstances, someone somewhere loves you. They may be long gone or be by your side right now. That is hardly relevant.

What matters is your ability to tune in and let their abundant love flow straight into your heart. For that is where our healing is to be found, first and foremost.

Close your eyes for a moment and ask for that radiant love to visit you and know that how it manifests is not as important as that it *does*.

Rest assured that you are loved. And so the rest of life is all beautifully up to you.

Are You A Spiritual Hitchhiker?
❦ October 27

RECENTLY I HAD a dream in which I was hitchhiking. Thumb out, I was letting the Universe carry me along a country road. I was confident a ride would show up at just the right time. Alternatively, I was terrified that no one would come and I would have to walk miles and miles to the nearest place of comfort.

This dream taught me that the choice is entirely up to me – that I could actually get where I was going either way. Reaching the destination happens either way; it's the quality of the trip that varies.

In the dream, when I was happy and confident, I could attract a ride and easily reach my goal. But when I was worried and anxious, help was nowhere to be seen and I slipped into that dark, dank place of Victimhood.

Then I imagined myself trudging along in the dark for hours. I saw myself as universally rejected by mankind – a loser, a tagalong, a wannabe unworthy of any kind of support. I was instantly filled with fear because the Universe was no longer my benevolent protector.

Enter the Victim.

I so don't want to be a Victim in this short life of mine – nor do I want to spend my time placing my needs at the feet of others as if I, myself, cannot meet them. I want to move confidently through this world – to be a universal traveler who can skip the drama and just get where I am going with infinite trust.

Teal taught me about hitchhiking, which she did all over Europe. She relied entirely on her gut as she traveled from country to country, sometimes alone and sometimes with others, via her thumb. Hitching rides taught Teal to trust her gut and her consciousness.

In her journals, she writes about the experience of sizing up the various drivers who stopped to offer her a ride along the way. Sometimes she said no and sometimes she said yes – the decision was made entirely in the moment based on the feelings that ran through her body.

Not only did Teal never make a wrong move, but she also got where she was going by implicitly learning how to say yes to herself. She was willing to put her own fears, along with her sense of lacking and her inner Victim, politely to the side. Instead of giving in to these voices, she listened to her great Inner Protector.

Not all rides are a good fit for us, and the results we desire are rarely guaranteed. Instead, we are given both the sweet and the bitter side by side as we continue to hone our sense of self-trust.

Do you trust yourself implicitly enough to get in a car with a "stranger" – driven by Spirit and the Universe – and be delivered to where you need to go? Even if you don't know exactly in your conscious mind how it will unfold?

Can you let go of the plan long enough to pick a destination and let right action flow through you? Can you feel your way with your body in the moment?

You are infinitely capable of utilizing that sense of rightness for yourself right here and right now. What do you wish to create that is just waiting for your healthy dose of self-trust? Where do you need to suspend the "how" and instead tune into the feelings in your body?

When you tune in to your infinite power, you wisely invest in love for yourself. And so the beautiful instruments of your body and soul become well honed.

The Power of Hard Decisions
꙳ October 31

IN LIFE WE are called sometimes to do seemingly impossible things, like leaving behind an old life that no longer fits. People will be hurt. We could be hurt. We will have to give things up that have long been a comfort. So we figure we just can't do it.

And, yet, if we don't proceed we know we will get stuck on life's path – unable to move forward or backward until we do that unthinkable thing.

I made exactly such a move two years ago, when I left my old life and moved across the country to San Francisco. I gave up being a wife, a hands-on mom, came out as a lesbian and left behind a business as an Internet marketing coach at the height of my success. It was basically every transition you could make all packed into one tidy package.

Believe me, it was anything but "tidy." Mistakes were made, hearts were broken, and many tears were shed. Yet I know I moved as consciously as I could at the time.

There just isn't any pain-free way to do these hard things. I was being called – as we all are sooner or later – to honor the tugging of my soul, pulling me along. My soul had been waiting for the right time to grow and expand – even if that meant giving up everything in my life that was trusted and comfortable.

One night around that time I had a dream in which my long deceased father showed me a street in San Francisco, near the home of my new business partner, Jeffrey, with whom I was starting a spiritual marketing business.

In the dream I suddenly blurted out, "I'm going to live there!" My father nodded, smiling.

Then he showed me the destruction of the World Trade Center and in that moment I experienced a wave of intense grief – what felt like all the suffering in the world. I fell to my hands and knees and began to vomit up matted pages of magazine text, my old cultural programming. That was when I knew I was meant to move forward and heal people – no matter what the cost would be.

Believe me, I had fears. Could I really trust the Universe to protect me, guide me and keep me safe as I changed my life? What if my new business partnership didn't work? What if I was wrong about being gay? What if I never found true love again? What if Larry and I couldn't come to a peaceable agreement around the divorce? What if my son became distant and angry with me?

What if no one wanted this new spiritual type of marketing that Jeffrey and I were crafting?

If I let them, worried thoughts of my imminent demise and the end of my happiness could have engulfed me. Yet there was a truth here; for this *was* the end of happiness as I knew it. Since then these worries have been replaced by a deep understanding that I am in the right place, at the right time, doing the right thing.

This path has not always been easy and joyful. But every piece of it has been right.

That is what alignment is all about. Your soul gets to the point of expansion where it simply can't live the old life anymore. Something has to give – whether it is your work, your relationship, your environment, or how you treat your body. And so you surrender to this calling or continue fighting it all the way.

Once you surrender completely life starts to really click along, showing you where to go each step of the way. You become lighter, more nimble, and better able to weather the storms that arise. You can now maximize each challenge as an opportunity – and your emotional grounding becomes stronger and more stable.

To do this we may have to face some dark stuff; this is natural. If we have no capacity for grief, then we have no capacity for life itself. We cut ourselves off from what we allow ourselves to be, think and feel. And so our zest for life simply gets drained away.

I want to live life absolutely – to know the zeal of an excellent day, the importance of deep friendships and the white fire of great love. I want to be consumed by my life – to get out of the way and let Spirit pour through me. I long to become a truly empty vessel, a container for deep love and joy.

And this is exactly what is happening now in my grief over Teal's death. I am starting to feel better and better, more and more connected to the divinity in Teal and in all of us. I am becoming more alive to the extraordinary presence – the God – in her death and afterlife.

If you are holding on to something too tightly, ask yourself if fear will be your master. Or will love?

Will acceptance and support for your own desires be the rule of the day?

Or will you drag a life or a body or a relationship that no longer fits around behind you, allowing the weight of old baggage to hold you back?

Your soul is whispering to you, telling you the truth. Will you listen?

Am I an Adult Yet?

November 6

THAT IS THE question I asked myself recently as the veils began to lift about some of my chronic problems.

The most remarkable thing about losing Teal has been the extraordinary clarity that has descended as I begin to see the truth about my life. It's as if God has turned on the halogen lamps and I can finally examine things for what they really are.

Those tricky relationships in my past? Turns out I was not only calling forth difficult people to love, but I was in a hazy fog of denial about it. I believed some people loved me more than they did – and I couldn't see how harsh they were to me. I also mistakenly believed that I would be "the one" to triumphantly turn them around.

As if it was even my job.

And my financial ups and downs? That's another area where I had a hazy grip on reality – fueled by a desire to stay small, hidden and dependent by not putting on my big girl panties and handling my money responsibly. Hence my general propensity to spend what I had, save little, and rack up paralyzing debts.

This is what we do when we are afraid of life: we remain lost in childish thoughts. We do this when we fear that we are no match for adulthood. We are just sure that we can't be trusted.

I was always a kid with a big imagination. I was also a sensitive girl who got teased mercilessly and cruelly throughout my childhood. Every day included a mortifying and uncontrollable descent into tears. I was afraid to go out the door every day to school.

And so I became afraid to trust myself – and anyone else.

I coped by pretending that I was invincible, in just the way children do. So I never thought of my future realistically. In my childish thinking, I could imagine that at any moment my empire would appear and I would be rich beyond my wildest dreams. Or that the project I was working on would take off and sweep the globe! The last place I want to be is in the present, which has rarely resembled an empire.

In fact, my habits were set up to prevent me from having all that abundance and satisfaction I craved. I didn't want to see what life was offering me, or what was required. Instead it felt better to pretend so I could just imagine my way to happiness.

I used to believe that attending to details, and handling my more mundane responsibilities was beneath me. Part of me thought that I was special. After all, I was a "creative type." Weren't we secretly exempt from all of that stuff? I thought I could just float through life and get around to these responsibilities when I was in the mood to deal with them.

That part of me also wanted someone else to do it – a big protective daddy or mommy who would swoop in and take care of *everything*. Like a housekeeper who does lifekeeping, too.

Where is the satisfaction in that?

Do we truly want to be thumb-sucking babies all our life and avoid the distinct pleasure that comes from saving up to buy our first car, home, or business? For me, this desire to hide has shown up as addictive behaviors. In this new clarity, I find myself being drawn to 12-Step work.

Yes, that would be addiction recovery. Turns out there are many types of addiction and many programs for them –

rooms full of people just like me who are willing to sit and talk for a while. And so I find myself beginning this work, finally humble enough to admit I have issues and work on them.

As adults, we are called to prove what we are made of, to forge the fiber of our character by overcoming life's obstacles. We are challenged to connect with others deeply, to open our hearts with compassion, and to give the gifts we were born to give.

If we're afraid of life, then we deny ourselves the chance to experience those ultimate adult satisfactions. Hiding from responsibility keeps us stuck, angry and, at times, completely hopeless. Going through life being afraid simply doesn't work; this strategy confounds us as we fail again and again to get what we want.

This is not to say we shouldn't have visions, dreams and positive outcomes in mind; in fact, we must. But those dear dreams must be tempered with right action as well as the courage and clarity to see what is. And so we discover what is needed next, next and next.

Instead of being stuck in dreamland, and its corollary, the endless complaints of Victimhood, we can take responsibility. We must work with the Universe in right flow – with light effort, divine guidance and a clear view of where we stand and what is needed.

There is so much power to be had in standing up for ourselves. In leaving the job we hate for a better one we have created. Or in walking away from the relationship that no longer feeds us – no matter how much we love that other person.

To get there, we have to tell the truth. We have to own what galls us in life because, nine times out of ten, we created it.

We are the architects of our own existence, like master chefs creating a great sauce. When we accept the full responsibility of that job – and create with all the best ingredients, the very best tools and a loving, empowered intent – then we discover bliss.

I feel like I am finally surrendering to being an adult. And it feels so good to be getting back home.

How about you?

A Word About Your Emptiness
November 14

BEHIND ALL THE shiny cars, buzzing cell phones, overflowing to-do lists and structured days designed to max our potential, we are empty.

We are small, lonely and afraid. And we pretend like hell that we are not.

This is what it means to be human at this particular moment in our history and our lives. And, honestly, we are doing the best we can because we are only just becoming brave enough to glimpse into the gaping maw that eats at our core.

The gaping maw is our own creation. It was born long ago of the idea that if we acquire the right "stuff," it will save us. If we get that magical equation right – career + love + two great kids + house + good neighborhood = bliss – then everything else will fall into place.

Truthfully, that is where the emptiness begins. The illusion is that we can find happiness in a structure we build around us – like a well-dressed cage that we force ourselves to live in.

What we long for is actually our own redemption. Behind all of our good intentions is the simple desire to be forgiven – by God, by mom and dad, and, most of all, by ourselves.

We desperately want to be good people who do the right thing. Yet, at the same time, we doubt our ability to do that. All we really want to know is that we are loved – and that we are lovable.

42 ‿ *Surrendering to Joy*

So we devote our time and energy to getting it right. But if we assume that we're unlovable, we must work extra hard to fool the rest of the world into thinking that we are.

Somehow you don't have it together, no matter how hard you try to look good. You don't have it dialed in quite right. You are disappointed – in your significant other, in the life you have set up and, most of all, in yourself. Some of this carefully constructed structure simply has to come down.

Oh, why on earth did you agree to any of this?

Enter the gaping maw.

It's scary. Yet what is on the other side of that painful realization?

Redemption. True, blissful, honest to God redemption. Once you allow that heartbreak to engulf you, and you surrender to it completely, then you can find peace and truly begin to create.

That is what is happening now as I grieve Teal and all that I have let go of.

After being pinned to the floor, I have finally surrendered to myself. I have been forced to look, in the clear light of day, at everything that hasn't worked in my life. Slowly and lovingly, I am picking up the pieces on the floor around me.

My sad heart has become my friend. Night after night now I climb into bed alone with genuine Joy. I can rest! I can snuggle with myself! I can journal, pray, contemplate and talk to Teal and God.

I can read great books that help me understand my emptiness and make peace with it. And I can take the time to imagine in vivid, glowing pictures just what I *do* want ... me, Suzanne. Gone is the need to please a million other ghosts. Now I use this sacred time alone to feed my own delicate dreams.

I have stopped running from that state of broken-hearted emptiness. And I have begun to let go of the terrible shame that there is anything broken about me to begin with.

Honestly, we are so afraid of the darkest corners of life. But having spent some quality time there recently, I am here to report they are not so bad.

Life is never black or white – it contains all shades of grey. It is up to us to find that shade we are in right now and appreciate the warmth behind its walls of steel. It is up to us to rest our cheek on its smooth surface and thank God for the opportunity to know, love and trust our own vulnerability.

Only then can we give ourselves what we long for most in life – to once again embrace our own tender state of Joy.

A Different Kind of Gratitude
ℭ⅏ November 20

AS WE ENTER into the official season of heart opening, I'd like to propose a new way to think about gratitude.

We are often taught that we must be grateful for what we are given – homes, toys, careers, relationships. And, indeed, there is a lot to be grateful for there.

Yet let's look beyond all of that for a moment. What if that gratitude extended to things unseen, invisible and often forgotten?

What if you and I were grateful for something as simple as the air we breathe? Or the way the sun comes in the window, or the shape the curtain makes as it is gently blown by the breeze? Or the way our body feels heavy and relaxed as we sit reading.

The very fabric of life is teeming with sensation, energy and a force field of love that is waiting for you to touch into it. All you have to do is stop, slow down and feel into it. Even if you have forgotten – it is there and it is yours.

You knew it when you were very young, when you had not been fully trained to want things insatiably. You found comfort in that subtle presence all around you and tuned in without even thinking about it. The fabric of life mattered to you.

Then you grew up, and life became increasingly complicated. There were things to do, places to be, obligations to fulfill, and all those dreams of yours had to be tended to, step by step.

All of which had to be fueled by your relentless drive to succeed. Or perhaps it was not so relentless. So you found yourself giving up, getting confused or burning out.

And here you are.

If you are like me, long ago you forgot to connect with the present moment and all of its promise. You tell yourself you can't make that connection because you are too busy trying to just get along.

This, friends, is how we get disconnected from ourselves. We think our minds are running the show and so we'd better damn well listen.

That's usually when life happens. Plans get dashed. Everything gets turned on its ear. And we are forcibly made to surrender to the here and now because we believe we have no other choice.

That's what happened after Teal died. I had to rearrange my plans dramatically. And I had to become present to what has happening right here, right now. The launch of my would-be business has slowed down to a tiny crawl as I finally let go and allow myself to just be. To heal. To feel. And to tune into the finely spun fabric of gold of the present moment.

My conscious mind fought this. Believe me. (*What ... me? Surrender? Never!*) Even though my heart was broken, I thought I could crawl on like the last-standing member of Survivor.

But what would the point be?

In truth, slowing down has meant feeling the immense pain of missing my girl. Yet this is the truth that is present now. And it has its own sacred beauty.

There is nothing to avoid. There is nothing to be afraid of. There is only the self-love inherent in stopping and listening, for that is where the greatest joy will ultimately be derived.

When I listen carefully enough, I can hear her. I can feel Teal's radiant energy pour through me and it is beyond comforting. It's actually healing.

And that is what is available for all for all of us – to surrender to the love that is right here, at this very moment, a whisper just slightly out of earshot.

You can only hear it if you are willing to totally stop for a while for no good reason. To rest in your own solitude and tune into the orchestra in your soul, waiting for you to conduct with love and care.

Can you give yourself the gift of not crawling on, heroically, in your own life? Can you stop pulling yourself further and further from your center as you do those tasks you believe will help you hang on?

Just let go. Let go and then feel the sails of God flying you forward in peace, ease and tranquility. That is the only rescue any of us can truly know. It requires surrender to that which is right here and right now. With nothing added.

You know you need to do this if, like me, you have an aching in the pit of your stomach that begs to be heard.

What I can promise you is a delicious release – even if you only let go for one day, one hour or even one minute. In that release is clarity, promise and the expansion of your soul.

You are meant to grow and find your way back to bliss. And this may well be the key.

Something to Think About When Others Annoy You

🐦 November 28

YOU – AND YOU alone – are responsible for your happiness.

That's shocking, right? Because THINK of all the good excuses out there that would prove otherwise. After all, our fellow humans can be terrible jerks sometimes. As can we.

People do heartbreaking things to each other – they lie, cheat, steal, manipulate and even murder. And, yet, not one of those things is inherently cause for unhappiness. Just as disasters and other cataclysmic events are not always tragedies either. (Bear with me here, for I can hear your questioning mind.)

I learned this when Teal died. Instead of folding up into a horizontal packet of pain, I've managed to stay pretty upright with the occasional lie down for a good sob.

And I maintain this is because I have not, for one minute, held her death as a "tragedy." To me, it just isn't.

Her death is a manifestation of what Teal wanted for herself on a soul level. As painful as her early departure may be for the rest of us, this death is part of the deal she worked out with God before this lifetime even began.

Mind you, I'm quite sure Teal never once thought to herself on a conscious level that it would be a good idea to die young. But seldom do we orchestrate such things consciously.

What Teal knew was that she wanted to help people – a lot of people. And she wanted to do it in a way that was innate, natural, and in true guided flow. She was willing to work with God in whatever way necessary to make that happen.

So here we are. And she is indeed getting just what she came (and left) for.

This is how it is with anyone whose behavior or choices torment you. They are not in this world to live up to your needs, desires or expectations.

In fact, they are only here to live up to their own – as are you.

We are all divine children of the Universe. In each lifetime, we are given infinite chances to script our own happiness. So when another shows up with a path that differs from our wishes, we must ask ourselves this: why should they be any different than they are?

Recently, I annoyed someone who was close to me. I got all tangled up in my neediness about something and burst into his day with a very poorly expressed request.

Lord, the drama I cooked up! I immediately felt terrible – and I knew I'd triggered his "stuff" because while he met my request, he ignored my apologies. In his own way, he was letting me know a line had been crossed – and that he needed a bit of time and space to recover.

Oh, how I needed to be put out of my writhing shame and guilt. I wanted his forgiveness NOW – and it was not forthcoming, dammit!

This is exactly when I saw – in Technicolor – how dependent I was on his response. Then, suddenly, I understood. I could graciously give him the space to show up just as he was – without needing to change a single thing.

And here's the magical part: In that moment, *I actually forgave myself.* I let myself off the hook and graciously acknowledged that sometimes life is intense, and I don't operate perfectly every single time. I realized that sometimes my emotions get the best of me and I blunder along.

As long as I take responsibility and acknowledge my wrongdoing, I can give myself a break for being human. And

I can give others one as well.

Everything relaxed the minute I saw this. I no longer felt hamstrung, waiting for his forgiveness. Instead I honored him for taking the time to do what he needed for himself, which felt quite whole and right.

This way of thinking opens up a new world of possibility, one in which we accept each other just as we are with nothing added. So we no longer have to manipulate, cajole, maneuver or manage others to get what we want. Instead we can provide it for ourselves.

In the past, my mind would have whirred and snapped angrily that my friend's forgiveness was not immediately given. My childish self would stomp her foot and say, "Hey! What about me? I apologized!"

That is a guarantee of nothing, other than the fact that I apologized. Being able to let go and let the other be, just as they are, is not only a sign of maturity, it is also a huge relief to your sensitive soul. And it's something you deserve to give yourself.

Hanging on to another's "wrong doing" and playing it again and again in our mind is merely demanding they squeeze through the sieve of our own unreasonable expectations.

And so those harsh demands are simply the cries of our own thirsty souls, wishing we would, in fact, give ourselves a break, too.

Are you up to the challenge of letting another – and most of all, yourself – off the hook?

I know I am.

Learning to Trust Again
🐟 December 7

ONCE UPON A time, long ago, you and I trusted people. We were childlike with wonder and awe at all the world had to offer. We believed in magic and expected the people around us, specifically the big ones, to be magical as well.

Then it turned out they were only human. And sometimes not even very nice humans. That's about the time our trust got replaced with despair.

In this brand new, ripped-wide-open, cleaned-out life I am now living, I notice my lack of trust and my infinite despair. It can be a wonderful place to curl up in and suck my thumb.

Even though I know it's the right thing to do, sometimes it's hard to trust God.

And yet that essential trust is the one precious thing I have. It's really all I have – and I dare say that's true for all of us.

I write this from the rented room in a house that is a far cry from the big, rambling house that I once lived in with my husband on Lake Champlain.

In between bouts of sobbing, I spend my days contemplating life. It's a far cry from the busy days I knew as a successful business coach.

Even my big bed, empty now except for me, has unaccustomed space. I'm substantially alone with no desire to change that for the first time in my adult life.

In all of this emptiness, I am being forced to trust in God like I never have before. Perhaps this is true for all of us right now.

Because no one out there is going to "save us" any more than the Tooth Fairy will be making deposits in our Roth-IRA accounts. Were I to meet Mr. or Ms. Right tomorrow, that still wouldn't save me from my emptiness.

Nor would it save you.

Only one thing can save any of us from the black pit of our despair – and that is our faith in something far more infinite, more gracious, and far more forgiving than any of us.

That grace is our ticket back home; it's the way to surrender to the infinite vagaries of life. For God can take a soul as pure, simple and compassionate as Teal. It's true. But the same God can also send me a message from her voice teacher when she was a student at the Berklee College of Music.

It's a message I only found recently, nearly four months after her death.

"... Teal was strongly into the blues. Though my impression of Teal was of a sunny, positive-minded person, she connected with blues through her compassion for other people's struggles. And this was what gave her blues interpretations such passionate authenticity ... Teal brought a powerful sense of joy to her music, and her greatest pleasure was sharing that joy with others. She sang with heart, soul, spirit, and total commitment."

The message is clear: In the pathos lies the joy. I am not meant to wallow in pain for the rest of my life, any more than you are – whatever your struggles may be. We are all meant to live like Teal did and celebrate the beauty inherent in that pain.

This is Teal's legacy, which I am living now as a result of her life and her death: It is safe to trust God. It always has been and it always will be. And it is safe to treat those around us with grace, courage and compassion – whether they be our teacher, our guide, or the stranger on the bus.

And so the miracle of life goes on.

To see Teal sing the blues, go to www.suzannefalter.com/ tealmusic

The True Nature of BFFs
⚭ December 13

YESTERDAY ONE OF my daughter's oldest friends, her original childhood best buddy Shana, died after being in a coma for six days. Like Teal, she collapsed with a cardiac arrest and never regained consciousness. Like us, her family had to make the agonizing decision to remove her from life support.

At such times, one has to wonder what's at play: Is there some grand design to such things? Why would two girls not even 24 years old be taken only months apart? And why would two who were once so close die such similar but completely un-related deaths? Perhaps the causes were different (Shana's cardiac arrest was caused by binge drinking), but how they unraveled in their last six days on Earth was exactly the same.

What is it about the invisible links we all share, the per-manent, on-going connections that tether us all? Not only were Shana and Teal dear friends, their brothers were close as well. And Shana's mother has been one of my own dearest friends for nearly 30 years.

Laurie and I were once gadabout girls in Big Advertising in New York who could live on Happy Hour hors d'oeuvres for days at a time. And, like our daughters, we both dreamed of being discovered some day – making it big in the calling of our dreams.

None of that matters so much now.

When Shana and Teal were little, they were the kind of friends who ran toward each other down Greenwich Village side streets, eagerly screaming each other's names in their boundless eight-year-old enthusiasm.

Once they were both in a professional play together. Shana played the lead and Teal was her understudy. For years afterward, they laughed about how Teal had left the prop teddy bear on stage in her one big performance and it sat there prominently throughout the next scene.

They were both Uno-playing card sharks who went to Spice Girls movies together and always managed to talk some parent into buying candy after the show. Then Teal moved to the country and Shana stayed in the city. Shana became an actress. Teal became a singer. The world beckoned and they answered, the strands of their dreams trailing behind them, weaving them together invisibly for the rest of life.

That is what happens to best friends. They drift apart but something always brings them back together.

No matter what passes between them in life, best friends always have a resonant tuning with each other. It's the result of all those hours and hours of shared Barbie dress-ups, or lovelorn conversations, or whatever their special magic is.

Some best friends stay forever – and some grow up and move on. Yet the resonant tuning remains. It is this way with all of our significant relationships.

We have soul links to all sorts of people that we can only guess at – they are invisible yet as invincible as the steel ropes pulling the cable cars up the hills of San Francisco.

That is why you and a dear friend can pick up twenty years later as if not a day had passed. And why Laurie and I have been fated to travel this incredible road together – of loving our girls more than life itself and then sitting by their hospital beds as they slowly slipped away.

This is the nature of our destiny. It is something we create with each person we touch. Our destiny is nothing more than the interweaving of lessons between lives.

Laurie teaches me as I teach Laurie – and our children teach us both. As do our mothers, fathers, employees, bosses, teachers, lovers, and even the guy who flips us the bird in rush-hour traffic. These people all around us are our everyday Christ figures – those in whom we see ourselves reflected. And so, moment by moment, we have the opportunity to grow.

I am learning a whole new level of compassion and humility from this experience. Destiny is not to be messed with. It is a mysterious force unto itself that cannot be understood or fully comprehended. Doing so is insignificant.

Instead, destiny is to be accepted and worked with, felt into and, ultimately, surrendered to. That is all any of us, with our limited mortal coils, can ever do.

What a privilege it was to know Shana, a beautiful spark of talent and sweetness. To know her in her gorgeous whirl with Teal, the two of them dancing through childhood with unfettered glee, was blissful. I can still see them walking down the street, hand in hand, and I am grateful for the experience.

That memory alone is enough to last a lifetime.

How the Worst Year of My Life Was My Rebirth

Ⱥ January 1, 2013

2012 WAS A watershed year for me – I let go of so much. And just when I was wandering aimlessly through the desert, not knowing who I was or where I was to go, I lost Teal.

This is when things started to get truly interesting. For I thought I'd been through "the worst" when this happened. I loved my partner! I was in anguish that she ended our relationship! And now where was I supposed to live? In truth, I was still reeling from the official end of my 25-year marriage, as well, and the arrival of my divorce decree.

And, hey, how was I going to make a living now anyway because that business ended as well? Oh, the drama, self pity and victimized howls of protest that ensued …

Then Teal died and tore the lid off all my preconceived notions about myself and what life is really all about.

Now I know that the "story" that we tell ourselves from day to day is meaningless. There is no right and no wrong, and no one can ever truly hurt me or you.

I write this with tears of gratitude streaming down my face, for what I do know is that we are always held in divine grace – we just are. And when we remember and turn back toward that comforting life, the answer is right there. And it's as clear as day.

So I have learned I am nothing more than a healer. The only thing that REALLY matters in this life is that I touch those I'm meant to touch.

How much you or I "have" is an illusion. I gave up the big showcase house a few years ago when I left my marriage and have been steadily downsizing every since.

Now in the sunny, beautiful room I rent, I have no mortgage, no love interest and no big obligations. I even gave up my smart phone in the interest of becoming more present and less distracted.

So I am discovering emptiness. And in that beautiful, simple place, I grieve, I let go more and more, and so I truly heal. I have begun to piece together the puzzle of my life, and in doing so I am finding a new picture of myself.

This picture of me is stronger, freer, and far more stable. I'm more grounded in what is right and true, and no longer needing to hang on tenaciously to that which does not serve.

I no longer need to prop up the false image I projected to the world for all those years, as the hero with all the answers. So I am no longer ready to fix any problem, leap into any fray, and hold up the Universe on my bony shoulders.

No, no, no. I have no answers for anyone, really. And I simply didn't realize the Universe wanted to hold *me* up. And so I can safely say that the "worst" year of my life was in so many ways my rebirth. My delivery. My redemption.

One of the sweetest discoveries is that I have friends! Like Sally Field receiving her Oscar, I'm just now seeing the big sea of caring souls out there who believe in me.

For the first time in my life, I am truly letting in that caring support and it is vast. I am embracing them all, from the total strangers whose stories weave and intermingle with my own in recovery groups to those who leave their naked, beautiful shares on my posts on Facebook.

Hundreds and hundreds of people from across the different decades of my life have contacted me since Teal's death, reaching out simply to say they are sorry I am in pain. New friends have arrived in my new world north of San Francisco, all of them committed to holding me and helping me through this.

So I dissolve, again and again, into the sweet bliss of union.

I talk to Teal often. She drops in at night when I waken sometimes. Lately the Bob Dylan song "I Shall be Released" has been playing in my head. So I looked up the lyrics, which explore seeing one's light come shining into the east. Which is when we shall be released.

I know I am in the process of being released into that very light. I am being shown the vast chambers within – my own sea of tranquility, my own gleaming horizon which I can venture toward. There is no other choice, is there?

I mean, yes, okay. You *can* mire yourself in the petty pursuit of being right and lock yourself in a cage of your own fear. And you can cling to all that is tangible as the "way" – putting the pursuit of security first before everything else.

Or you can simply surrender, let go and slide down the waterslide of Spirit into bliss. As someone who is doing exactly this, let me reassure you that the water feels just fine.

May you discover just how held you are – how beautifully, preciously loved you are –by those around you, by God and even by the rest of us.

Discover that oneness by simply letting go. For that truly is your ticket to peace.

How to Forgive Your Mother
ᐸᐸ January 8

I SAID GOODBYE to my mother a few days ago. At ninety-four, she is a fragile, shrunken figure lying in a nursing home bed, a once-fierce woman who has lost her ability to speak. A former magazine columnist, she can't think much these days beyond the spot on her trousers or the nail polish she keeps chipping from her fingers.

Boo is waiting to die, though death as a concept is not something she understands anymore. She just knows she is waiting for something, and the wait seems very, very long.

When I sat with her each day in her room, she knew who I was – at least I think she did. She gave me that special look reserved for mothers and their daughters – a combination of pride mixed with assessment. "I love your sweater," she managed to say. It was the only sentence she spoke.

Boo was a blue-eyed Campus Queen of Stanford, class of 1940, who married one of the few men around during World War II. He was dashing; she was beautiful. She was profiled in *House Beautiful* as a perfect wife and mother, despite the fact that she was in the middle of leaving her glamorous husband and fleeing east with another man.

Her three children got to come along, too.

How to write about my mother and the mille-feuille of our complicated relationship? Imagine layer upon layer of shame, guilt, fear, dedication, devotion, control, jealousy, empathy, strategy, maneuvering, and, yet, ... somehow ... still love.

Then imagine me – loud, precocious, smart, too much and completely unexpected after she remarried. And picture her – anxious, worried, overwhelmed and trying desperately to get it right in her new marriage.

And then soak it in a whole lot of booze and pills. Throw in a suicide attempt, weekends in Manhattan, lots of celebrities, loud fights and an ever-expanding attempt to keep the glamour going in her Liz Taylor-Richard Burton style marriage to my father.

Somehow there was love all stitched under, through, and around the chaos.

My mother speaks to my soul in some basic way that only mothers can. Long ago I managed to detach from needing her seldom-dispensed approval. And I learned how to not ask for help over the years because she always turned the conversation back to herself. But she is still in my heart.

So I'd be a liar if I said I didn't have resentment; Boo was far from the perfect mother. Yet there is that damn love. When one is near death, that is really all that matters.

With it comes the opportunity for forgiveness. Because these days there doesn't seem to be much charge around my "story" of Boo's misdeeds. In fact, it bores me silly.

There is only the present. Time has stripped her bare and there is only a coming to terms with its march, ever forward. I have no need to bear a grudge any more. I am my own creation now – not my mother's, despite her many failed attempts to get me back in the box I kept slipping out of.

While I sat by her bed, she spent much time just looking at me. Sometimes she eyed me suspiciously from the depths of her dementia. More often, she just gazed at me serenely. We sat in Zen silence and communed.

There really was nothing to say; it was just a state of being to hang out in. And so this visit was extraordinarily tender and intimate in its own sweet way.

The drama had melted away. Life had become basically insignificant, rendering us mute.

Near the end of the visit, I apologized to my mother for not coming to visit her more often over the years. She lives in the suburbs of Philadelphia and I live in Northern California so visits have only happened occasionally for some time. I cried and felt genuine remorse. Truthfully, I stopped trying to be a good daughter decades ago.

She just gave me a look that dismissed all of my concern, my shame, and my neglect in a heartbeat. It doesn't matter, she seemed to say. Boo understood.

That's when it sunk in that I would probably never see her again. This was it. The thought filled me with a deep clutch of grief.

Before I left, I gave my mother a hug and held her close for a long time. Then, for a moment, I stroked her cheek. Her eyes softened and there it was – that damn love beaming out at me. Whether she knew me or not didn't matter any more. I knew she loved me deeply.

In the face of such love, all anyone can do is just lay down their sword. And so it was that I came to forgive my mother.

And that she forgave me.

Learning to Forgive Myself
∝ January 15

I AM LEARNING to do the unthinkable these days: I am learning to forgive myself. This is not a purchase that is easily won.

Getting there requires doing something most of us avoid. I have to look at my transgressions, those little things I did that made me stink. I have to go right into the belly of the beast.

Addiction recovery programs refer to this as making "a searching and fearless inventory" of ourselves and then admitting to God, to ourselves, and to another person exactly what we did wrong.

I've been using 12-step recovery groups as my unofficial grief group, for these are my people. But how I have resisted this kind of work for it requires I acknowledge that I am flawed. The mask of perfection I've carefully paraded through this life is cracked and must be removed.

Perhaps you know that mask.

It's that sense that at any given moment, in any given situation, you'd better damn well have some answers – whether you know anything about what's going on or not. No wonder addicts are born this way.

How I have carried the weight of the world on my shoulders all these years, needing to prove to others how worthy I am. Your problem becomes my problem, my test of strength, my proving ground. And if I solve it, will you love me?

There is no valor here as it turns out. There is only neediness and grasping. There certainly is no love.

There can't be. For in this place, my well has run dry. I have no love for me so there won't be any for you either.

Wildly enough, there is this new place of possibility that lives smack dab in the middle of my weaknesses. In this place, I am learning to breathe again, to relax and be gentle with myself.

I am seeing that old need to control, cajole, push, manipulate, steamroll and otherwise persuade others to do things "my way" wasn't okay. But it also wasn't my fault.

It was simply a way of being that was firmly locked in place by the time I was five years old – and it had a lot to do with survival.

Back in those days, I listened to a lot of fights at night as I was trying to go to sleep. My martini-laced parents would be at it again, their voices raised as they hurled accusations like hand grenades, while I lay in my bed hugging myself and humming to avoid the incredible fear that at any moment my world would end.

They had divorced other people before. They could do it again. And then where would I be?

When we are young, we assume things. We assume we are responsible. We assume we must put out the fires. We assume that if we don't do this, we will die. And sometimes, we are even right.

Most of all, we assume we don't rate the usual love – the kind that's unconditional.

Now, all these years later, the ghosts in the corners still want to be fed. They are tapping us on the shoulder, saying, "Please look at me! Please feed me."

If we are in the second half of life, it's now or never, as our ghosts remind us.

So I am carefully taking out these weaknesses of mine one at a time and examining them like fine china in an antique shop. I am studying their cracks and their patterns, and observing their innate beauty. In these weaknesses, I see a map of my pain.

I am no longer afraid of what I will find because it doesn't matter as much. While losing everything in the past year, I learned the freedom of non-attachment.

Since I am no longer trying to hang onto a dying marriage or a toxic relationship, or a business partnership that is past its prime, I am free to explore. And since I no longer have a big world to support, I don't have to be impressive. Or smart. Or even well-packaged.

All I have to be is me. And, right now, that means giving myself the time and space to own my copious transgressions. In the process, I can see the sweet, childish logic that kept them in place for so long.

I used to think my problems were the meanies who came after me – those taunting kids at school; my erratic, troubled mother; and, later in life, lovers who judged me harshly and rebuked me with stinging verbal assaults. Man, were they *wrong.*

But who invited them in to play? I did, back when I was little Susie. And why? Because of what she endured as a little girl who lay in her bed all those years ago, humming and hugging herself, avoiding the truth that life wasn't always safe. And because she believed that she didn't deserve love.

I have immense sympathy for little Susie now. She did the best she could, albeit clumsily.

Now I can slowly let my shoulders relax. Tenderly, I can acknowledge that I am no longer being tested and I can take myself off the hook.

Perhaps I can even set up a new life for myself in which love is no longer shot through with harshness, but kindness.

And I can find that freedom I have longed for all these years – the freedom to love myself again, and so love another as deeply as I can.

Isn't that what the promise of life is all about?

How clever of God to hide this bliss in the one place we are least likely to look: our most awkward, unkind moments. If we can love ourselves there, then we can love the world as we were intended to – freely, beautifully and fully.

Spending the Weekend with God

 January 19

TODAY I AM having a daylong date with God. Maybe I'll even make it a weekend with God. I have no plans and no particular place to be – only some vague ideas about laundry, a swim, and maybe a pedicure.

So I surrender. I choose to be in that divine place of un-certainty on the edge of reasoned thought. In this minute, at least, I don't need to fill myself with tasks. Or even to know what I'm going to do next.

Oh, the glory of nothing to do! How I feel I can let my-self relax and open up to new possibilities. I'm like a tightly closed bud, unfurling in my own time.

Those of us who are alone – the divorced, the widowed, the lonely, the unattached – often dread weekends. That is when you go to The Home Depot and see couples walking the aisles, shopping for sinks and paint. If you're grieving the loss of a child like I am, you see children darting here and there. And you long for your little girl, the young woman who no longer exists

Just for the record, I don't want a partner, a home, a reno-vation project, or even another child at this moment in my life. But I can remember spending more time in longing than in contentment, when the rest of the world seemed to grasp this "life thing" far better than me.

Then I used weekends like a weapon. They were my acid test: Did I have it together enough to fit in with the weekend-happy crowd of relationally successful people? Could I pull off this thing called a happy life?

There's another question on my mind today: Can I let myself off the hook and just embrace where I am right now?

Can I allow myself to love my aloneness and the expansive, rich, creative palette of possibilities spread out before me? Can I actually wake up, like I did this morning, be excited about life, get going and see what I can discover?

Can I allow myself to not know what will unfold on this date with God? Can I give myself joy as a gift today, instead of yearning?

Can I trust myself enough to dissolve into contentment just like I swim in the lap pool up the road, lap after lap, with no limit and no end?

Can I know I am worth trusting again? Even though I blew it repeatedly in ways imperceptible to anyone else's eye over the years and even though I've been left with my lot of pain, can I emerge, blinking into the sunlight?

I'm fool enough – or possibly wise enough – to believe that God wants to spend the weekend with me. And so I make my aim to be good company, in that I will listen more than I speak.

I will soften more than push.

And above all, I will tune into my desires moment after moment. And give myself just what each moment calls for.

What are you doing this weekend for yourself? For your soul?

What if There Really Was Enough in This Sweet World?

❧ January 23

LATELY I'VE BEEN thinking about my future. This is a place that we divorced women go to often in our minds.

Will I have what I need as I get older? Can I create a big enough safety net? And can I really rely on just me to provide whatever I need for the rest of my life?

These are practical questions that must be asked. Somewhere long ago, I was programmed to believe that others should take care of me. Sensing that I wasn't enough, I believed I couldn't do it alone.

Maybe you know this feeling. It's a deeply grounded sense of lack. I've often felt like I was "just barely hanging on" no matter how many thousands of people read my books, no matter how many radio and TV interviews I book, and no matter how much money I make or how many gazes follow me around the room at cocktail parties.

I've been grateful for my accomplishments, mind you. But they were simply never enough to fill the gaping void at my core. This is the void that alternately screamed and whispered epithets, none of which were particularly nice.

It is really difficult to hear that voice. At the same time, it is impossible to ignore it. That voice springs from the very core of our being, a place where we know ourselves like no one else does.

This becomes the voice with which we can build – or not build – our future.

Enter a sense of lack. This is the quality my own inner voice has feasted on for years. In my own childlike way, I tried to keep up with its demand for more.

I hired lots of experts who knew more than me and I wound up in debt more than once. I made agreements with business colleagues I couldn't keep. I waved my little flag of shame right alongside my wins. Yet my insatiable, gaping maw still was not satisfied.

It devoured every win I had and then immediately smacked its lips, requiring more. No matter how hard I tried, I could never keep up.

For a long time it seemed like there wasn't enough in this world of whatever I wanted – be it money, love or vacation days. But in my heart a slower truth burned: I simply was not "enough" nor would I ever be.

The illusion of lack perks along, telling us again and again things that are just not true. In fact, we are enough. We were born enough. We have always been enough. And we will always be enough. God designed us this way.

It is only that seed of self-doubt, planted by our sweet, simple, childish minds that leads us to believe otherwise. From this seed our learning path is carved, step by rocky step.

The answer is not to shake ourselves by the shoulders and bully our souls into submission, demanding better behavior. You may have noticed, as have I, that that strategy does not work.

Incredibly, we must make friends with the hungry, gaping maw.

We must own that diminished dark place inside that sucks in all scraps of goodness and spews out toxic waste. We simply need to muster up our courage, shine the light on the maw and get to know it better.

When we do that, we learn a surprising secret: The maw is there to protect us. That's all it wants.

How could something so vengeful, so personally hateful, be motivated by love? Because when we were one or two or three years old, our little child selves decided that this was so.

Almighty Mommy couldn't possibly be out of line, we thought, so we ourselves must be wrong. And so the maw appeared, creating the eternal condition of not-enough.

Again and again, we choose situations to bear that out.

This is part of the contract we make with the maw. Its job is to keep us on the edge of reason at all times, never comfortable and always grasping.

If we're really paying attention, we can begin to find our way out of trouble. We can learn from the signposts along the way and start to converse with the maw instead of simply feeding it.

We can begin to discover what we need. We can recognize our patterns. We can own our truths. And we can begin the dear, deep process of self-forgiveness.

So we rescue ourselves and finally begin to know "enough," in all of its tender, sweet, undiminished brightness.

Here is the peace that passes all understanding. And may it be yours today – if you so choose.

Turns Out You CAN Meet Your Own Needs...Who Knew?

 February 15

AH, LIFE.

Recently, it has taught me a lot about my own failings. For instance, that big suitcase of anger I've carried around most of my life? Boy, has it gummed things up for me.

But here is the good news! I can put that large, heavy valise down now. I don't have to carry it anymore. And as I do that, I can stop expecting others to save me.

Perhaps you can relate. I have a friend; let's call her Dawn. She is struggling. Like me, she's been through a huge transition in the last few years. It's one of the things that drew us together.

Dawn has certainly been a support to me since Teal died. And her support shows up in potent spurts, all of which I have drunk up thirstily – and I kept wanting more.

But more was not forthcoming because Dawn is struggling, too. So she has become a powerful teacher for me. Recently we went through a spate of planned get-togethers, all of which got cancelled, changed, rearranged. Man, was I pissed, even though I had done some of the rearranging myself.

Oh, that heavy valise of anger. I can feel its weight pulling on me as I drag it from room to room, town to town. And, oh, that craving for someone else to fix me.

Meanwhile, I forgot that the third stage of grief is anger because, hey, I'm a spiritual chick. I don't "do" mad. Except that I do sometimes, inappropriate white-hot flames as if I was a dragon. My anger has, at times, been my nemesis.

And now Elizabeth Kubler-Ross wants me to own my anger. Express it! Revel in it! That task seems impossible. But if I don't, I can't fully grieve the loss of Teal. The thought makes my toes curl.

So it becomes abundantly clear that my beef isn't with Dawn at all. It is with the fact that God has taken my beautiful daughter and I will never see her again. And, yes, that makes me mad. So woe to anyone who gets in my path right now and doesn't give me just what I want.

See what a fine teacher my anger is?

Harriet Lerner says in her excellent book, *The Dance of Anger*, that our anger is a critical warning system and not to be ignored. Nor is it to be vented willy-nilly. Rather, it is meant to be worked with, learned from, respected and understood. And savored, as well. Anger is a beautiful indicator that something is amiss – and that would be something in MY camp, not the other person's.

For instance, why must I demand that a friend who is struggling just as much as I am prop me up? What a disservice that is to poor Dawn and to me. It is most certainly not her responsibility to make me feel better. What can I do to get my needs met instead of having to place them at Dawn's feet?

"Yeah, yeah, yeah," my mind protests, "but you lost your kid." But what's so righteous about me that my pain is greater than hers, or anyone else's? That thought is just as untrue as the notion that it's up to Dawn to save me.

Losing Teal has been very rough indeed. Losing a child is the worst thing that can happen to a person, according to experts. But I maintain that we are all in this same leaky ship together. All of us have pain – just as all of us have the chance to turn it all around. And no one's pain is greater than anyone else's, for we all have different capacities for coping.

So, once again, Teal's death has been my deliverance, my

redemption. It's given me a chance to live a whole, rich, unencumbered life – one in which I am finally free to let go of the anger and love the world unconditionally. I can give the Dawns of the world a big, fat break. Instead of resentment, I can offer her a little compassion and some understanding.

Just as my girl once did when she walked the earth.

What a profound teacher Teal was in that way. She loved the world and all of its inhabitants fully, without reservation. She just did; it was in her bones. Would she have put up with my little angry snit about Dawn for one minute? Certainly not!

I can see her rolling her eyes right now, hands on hips, and saying, plaintively, "*Oh, come ON, Mom ...*"

I feel her reaching through from the afterlife, guiding me to let it go. So I get to reboot and live authentically. Not as a "nice person" who must hide my densely packed valise of anger at all times, but as a real person who can finally own her anger, learn from it, and give herself a break in the process.

I am not a saint. I'm just a person. I'm weak, vulnerable, and no longer eager to please – nor am I silently resentful.

Instead I am learning to have a little compassion for myself first and then others. And not because it's going to get me somewhere. In fact, there is nowhere to get.

As Teal knew, there is only love and understanding – a concept I am only just beginning to grasp.

Letting Go of Boo
꩜ February 25

LAST WEEK, EXACTLY six months to the hour after Teal died, my mother joined her. Boo's death was entirely different. It wasn't radical, like Teal's death. Instead, it was a gradual disintegration of a life, the slow drift of a continent.

It seems as if my mother had been dying much of her adult life. Boo was always craving a rest, a peace she just couldn't get. No matter how many lists she made from her bed while propped up on pillows, her Blue Willow coffee cup beside her.

No matter how many dinner parties she threw, no matter how shiny the antique copper pots were, no matter how perfect her hair, how straight her hems and how well-applied her lipstick, my mother felt like she just couldn't get it right.

Oh, but I am here to say that you could, Mom. You really could. And you did.

This is the secret children know that mothers seldom realize: You are far more loved and appreciated than you know.

Boo suffered from depression, anxiety, and a number of addictions. And through it all, as dark as it got, she still managed to be funny and elegant.

She dated Joe Kennedy, John F. Kennedy's brother who died in World War II. She dated Najeeb Hallaby, who went on to be the father of Queen Noor. She was Stanford's Campus Queen of 1940.

She was an early Martha Stewart, creating and writing "The Happy Housekeeper" for House & Garden Magazine.

It was the longest-running column in Condé Nast's history. And she was married to my father, a well-known artist, for 24 years. Along the way, she was also married to two other men named John.

Boo was an impeccable dresser and a great beauty. She loathed exercise, preferring great conversation accompanied by a few vodka martinis. She was a spectacular cook, and she knew how to jitterbug. About every twenty years or so, something would happen that would bring her to the edge of death. And every time Mom would magically survive.

I loved my mother more than anything. But I was also scared for her. At any moment, I felt like she could crumble, and that it was up to me to keep this fragile pastry shell together.

So I did what I could all through my childhood to help my mommy hang on. I never got mad. I always made my bed. I tried to be quiet and helpful. I made her endless little pictures of princesses, cats, and of her. They always said, "I love you Mommy!"

The pattern continued right through my twenties. I was the one teenager on the planet who didn't rebel. I let her pick out all of my clothes, although we did go to war over bell-bottoms. (She relented.) I remember one memorable lunch in the months leading up to my college graduation. Boo looked at me over her glass of Chardonnay and declared that I would go into "communications." Hearing that, I promptly burst into tears.

I didn't want to go into 'communications'! I wanted to be a Broadway star! I wanted to sing and act. I wanted to be a wild creative soul writing books in Paris. I didn't even know what "communications" was, but I felt as trapped as I'd ever been. And I'd be damned if I would go there.

God bless Boo. I understand now that she was just trying to be helpful.

What a folly it is to think our parents should be any way other than exactly how they are. This is why we chose them – for within all that pain they show us what we're made of.

I have done just what I wanted to with my life. Even though it meant that my mother and I didn't speak for months on end sometimes. I took risks again and again that kept me worrying in the night, almost none of which I ever told my mother about.

I was a big, loud, blast of energy in her life; too much for her, really. She was anxious, small and reserved, a woman trained to fit in, be charming and find her man.

No matter what.

In Boo's world view, it was always best not to rock the boat – this was true of so many women in her generation. And so she was ill-prepared to raise this maverick child.

Honestly, I think I scared my mother just as much as she scared me. Through her attempts to smother me with protection and to shape me into something more conventional, my mother actually set me free.

She gave me something to chafe up against, and so sharpen my wits and my will. Perhaps without even realizing it, my mother made me who I am today.

Within the great matrix of human understanding, we are given exactly those conditions we need to thrive – even if that thriving means we must spend a significant part of our life in pain.

Beyond the perimeter of that pain is a glowing field of redemption; it's a place we only allow ourselves to wander when we are ready. Once we're there we can finally take responsibility for our lives. And isn't that what leads us directly back to Joy?

Did Boo make mistakes? Yes.

Did I make mistakes? Definitely.

But none of that matters now. All that remains is the Unified Field of Love that unites us all.

In the last years of her life, dementia overtook Boo and all of her anxiety and insecurity melted away. She became extraordinarily present, and she was so very, very happy to see me each time I visited. This was the heart of our connection – that love that was always there, hiding underneath it all.

Forgiveness, as sweet and pure as local honey, flows back to us from the afterlife, no questions asked. And what I feel now is my mother's purest love and pride at the person I have become.

I was singing as I drove yesterday, and I could feel Boo drop in and join me. "That's right, Susie," she seemed to say. "Sing! Sing as loud as you want!"

Thank you, Mother, for everything. You will always be my greatest teacher. Most importantly, you were my mom.

And I will always love you.

How DO You Actually Love Yourself Again?
❧ May 1

FOR ME, THIS question has burned for years. I want fast and easy answers, but there aren't any to be found.

How I want to just flip a switch, but the switch cannot be flipped. I honestly want to begin to love myself more, but perhaps this is a slow process of natural reclamation, like renovating a big Victorian house with a lot of rooms that need replastering.

So I go about my redemption slowly, one room at a time. Right now I'm dealing with shame; I have a lot of it. I'm ashamed for every time I snapped at someone. I'm ashamed of everything I ever did that made someone mad. The list seems endless.

But my shame is slippery and hides under rugs and behind walls. I scarcely sense it is there, until some memory swims up to the surface and sears itself into my brain.

I think about an angry coming-of-age novel I published in my twenties that included some unkind descriptions of actual people. It was the kind of unthinking, brash thing you do when you're determined to make your mark at any cost. People read these words and people were hurt. And I wrote them – even though I was ridiculed and bullied endlessly throughout grade school.

The last thing I have ever wanted to do is hurt or humiliate another person publically. But I did.

Now, thirty years later, I want to go right back into the rotisserie to baste in more remorse. I want to shame myself as

I have always shamed myself, carrying my guilt like a heavy lead weight. Because, well, because I'm defective. But don't tell anyone, okay?

This is the shame that lurks behind my smiling, confident self you see in the pictures. I suspect that on some level it is shame that many of us share, which is not to say it's right or wrong. Our shame simply is, and it guides us like a rudder through life, pushing us forward on some river of our own determination.

Will we make things easy or hard for ourselves? Will the result be abundant or meager? Will we stew silently in our invisible cages of suffering, which we craft to keep the world at bay?

Because here is the truth about shame: It is a powerful place to hide. As long as I am ashamed of who I am, I cannot make a contribution and use my talents to serve others as fully as possible.

So right now I'm under repair, and I feel like I'm making some progress.

Here's the divine joke to all of this: When I wrote that novel all those years ago, I was motivated by a base desire to become "a star." I honestly thought it was going to make me famous, which now seems plain old naive, not to mention completely beside the point.

I thought by becoming a young literary star, I would somehow spruce up these damaged goods. Then I would be acceptable – loved, perhaps, even by those who had rejected me. Steadfastly, I ignored my reviews. I couldn't look. What if the critics didn't adore me? My plan would be ruined!

Instead I threw myself into promoting the book, and even managed to get it written up in a few high-profile magazines. This was really going to "make" me, I thought.

I had wild imaginings. Parades in my honor! Invitations

to speak to thousands! And, of course, a spot on Oprah's couch. At the end of the day, however, my publisher shredded 4,000 unsold copies of the 7,500 that had been printed. My book was declared a dud.

So my novel disappeared, leaving behind a trail of shame, disappointment, and the wagging finger in my mind that persists to this day.

The good news is that all these years later, forgiveness is in sight. I now understand that I am not the results I achieve. I also understand that I'm not perfect and I don't need to be, nor do I need others to stamp me with their seal of approval.

Most importantly, I am starting to accept the fact that I make mistakes. If I pay attention, I can actually allow myself to grow from them.

Being a star now feels like a childish dream. Now my entire being wants to focus more and more on what is here now, in this moment. What is asking to be shared? Created? Loved? Noticed and appreciated?

And who am I being asked to be? Right here and right now? I have begun to listen closely.

I have a new prayer which I picked up from the wonderful documentary, *Raw Faith*. In it, a minister says her daily prayer to God: "What's next? I'm available." It is in this simple question that I can find my way back to true peace and joy. Feeling my way along the Braille trail I go, straight toward my redemption.

As I do, I forgive myself just a little bit more. Finally, in God's love and understanding, can I find my own worthy self.

And you know what? She's not so bad at all.

Is This Crazy Contraption Seriously Going to Work?

⤫ May 10

SEE IF THIS SOUNDS familiar.

You write a book, build a business, take a job or create something based on guidance, a hunch, or a screaming instinct that you have. You do it because you know – *you really know* – you are meant to do this thing.

But in the back of your mind there is also doubt. It feels squeamishly tender. You are scared, dammit! Do you seriously have to do this thing? Really?

This is where I find myself as I emerge as a changed woman with a permanently changed offer to the world.

I'm talking about my writing. A book is slowly accumulating steam, patiently biding its time. It seems to be lodged somewhere in my veins, waiting for the moment when I'll open one and write.

One rule of the Universe I know by heart is that if I'm not clear on my transformation – and I can honestly stand behind its value – no one will be. I must own the power of this emerging work down to my toes.

And like anyone facing their deepest truth, I'm scared. It's not that I fear I can't sell a book or make my living from this work; I've proven in the past I can do that. It's more that I fear the tender, deeply vulnerable rightness of this work, and the place I have to go to produce it.

I fear the raw power of what I experience every time I sit down and put my hand in that flame.

It's as if every step of my life has prepared me for this point. From my days studying art history and learning how to really look at things and write about them, to my stints as copywriter, failed novelist, and guided self-help author the first time around.

Yet, it is mostly Teal's death that has prepared me for this work. From the moment I stood looking at her stretched out before me on the hospital bed, encased in tubes, wires and monitors, I knew the moment had come.

I knew she would die and that I would be forced to be re-born. I knew the truth was finally going to have its way and, for once, I could not stop it. Like all of us at that moment of truth, I was ripped wide open and all the falsehoods in my life were wiped clean at once.

This burning away is a process we all must succumb to one way or another. Perhaps it happens through the end of a marriage or the loss of a job. Maybe it happens with the death of a parent, a serious illness, or the bottoming out of an addiction that has to end.

Sooner or later, all of us must fall off the apple wagon of our own pretentions and dissolve into the nothingness that God requires. To fight it is nothing less than pure folly.

We are transient beings on this planet and we are here for one purpose alone – to experience our own sweet, tender fragility and gain strength in its expression. We have to know this truth and surrender to it fully, letting it show us the way.

Most of all, we have to trust the deep and lasting value of what is born anew. It's the old "Sally Field problem" – we are being called to know our value in the world.

Yet somehow we are wired for complete denial of that fact. When Michelangelo was working on the Sistine Chapel, he wrote in his diary, "I am no painter!" Mark Twain wrote of his classic *The Adventures of Huckleberry Finn*: "I may very well pigeonhole it or even burn it."

Our reticence around our truth turns out to be quite normal. And I have to just keep reminding myself of this fact as I cycle back down to writing once again.

There is always perfection in God's plan for us. You can trust it and so can I. We may feel overly sensitive along the way, but that is how it is to be stretched as we grow.

All that is required, ultimately, is our willingness. Are we willing to surrender and "face the music" of our own discontent? Can we allow ourselves to find the path back to our deeper truth, our purest voice?

I, for one, can only say yes. How about you?

The Very Temporary Nature of Suffering
May 30

SUFFERING SEEMS TO be all around me these days. Oh, yes, I almost forgot: I see how I suffer, too.

One friend is angry at her dentist. Another is furious with her former spouse. What Spirit is showing me more clearly than ever is that this suffering and resistance we cook up time and time again is both critical and temporary. It's simultaneously a fearsome reality and a grand illusion.

In truth, our suffering is nothing more than an excuse to check out and play small for a while. Honestly, we may need it on some level. For we plug into our pain just like a lamp enjoys a socket. We literally become electrified with fear, greed, envy, hatred, resentment, anxiety, terror, panic and lust for all that we believe we cannot have.

We become consumed by these emotions until the moment we decide to look up – and then somehow it all starts to lift.

Teal was a big one for moving through these stormy seas quickly. Even as a very small child she would have her rant. Then, just as suddenly as it came on, she would give her little shoulders a shake and move straight back to joy.

I used to quietly admire this quality of hers, for she was 100 percent authentic in her upset. There would be a panic that her math homework wasn't going well and she would flunk a test. Or when she was older, there might be a tearful breakdown around "what the hell I am doing with my life."

Grief would rattle through her at warp speed, and there was something healthy about it.

We used to laugh that she needed to have her "two-week cry." Every couple of weeks, pretty much on schedule, Teal would call me up and have a cry about amorphous things. Sometimes it would even be about nothing at all; she just needed to cry. I'd listen and she would move through it. Then her usual radiance would come streaming back.

So Teal taught me about the temporary nature of suffering – for it was always with great grace and apparent ease that she moved in and out of her pain. Never once did she cling to it because she thought it would get her something or because she "needed" it. She expressed her sadness simply because it was there.

How easy it is for us to assume there will be some kind of reward or payoff at the end of our suffering. For me, that shows up as: "*So and so is really going to pay this time!*"

Yet there is no reward, just as there is no justification.

For many years I labored hard in the mines of advertising as an underpaid and, I thought, unappreciated junior copywriter. Day by day I wrote ads for things like "Doan's Little Back Pills." Then I'd walk away at 5 o'clock hating my work, hating myself and convinced this life I'd created was all a big mistake.

In these sad years, I told myself I could do no better, that I somehow needed this ill-suited job. And so I forgot God's most sacred principle: We are all divine in our ways, and when we force ourselves to hang onto something that doesn't fit, it's a sacrilege.

This is the thing that I notice again and again these days. That suffering can be a choice, like a punishment we feel we have to be oddly loyal to. In this way, I felt I had to stay in the love relationships in which I suffered and hung on month after difficult month.

All of it fed my persistent, dogging sense of shame at the time. And so it is with all prolonged suffering. We hang on rather than walk away because we mistakenly believe it's all that we've got.

But it's not, friends. In fact, it's far from it.

Only by making the conscious choice to let go of the pain and swim back to wholeness can we move ahead, tiny snail-inch by snail-inch. Isn't that the purpose of our slow crawl here on Earth?

The point of life and all of its hurdles isn't to prove anything to anyone. It's to discover, leaf by leaf, and to unfold, petal by petal.

The purpose of our struggle is to set us right again, simply by learning to maneuver through life.

Only by wading through the pain to the other side can we finally, actually grow. So we right the child within us who was abused. In doing so, we discover compassion for ourselves and the world.

It is in setting our minds to reclaim our wholeness that we build our most effective strategy for life. That wholeness demands that we let go of our suffering. So I become more and more aware of my own fragile little cages of pain, and I let go of them, one by one.

Once released, through prayer, meditation, and sometimes through forgiveness and making amends, they transform into flowers lifting into the sky. No longer needing to serve any earthly purpose, they disappear and are forgotten.

So I find I can stand a little taller and stretch a little further, empowered once again by the grace of God flowing freely through my veins.

It feels good to be alive.

Lifting the Veil on Mom
June 5

THE OTHER MORNING, as I lay awake in the post-dawn light, a dream fragment meandered through my mind. I saw my mother's favorite Liberty scarf, one she gave me, with a hole worn clean through it.

It was not a big hole. It had not been cut or torn; it looked like a picked-at, worn-through sort of hole.

And it was not the work of mice or moths. It was the work of my greatest undertaking: restoring my self-esteem after my mother's petulant, erratic care.

I am not here to point fingers and assign blame to a woman, now dead, who did the best she could with skimpy emotional means. Yes, I'm pissed right now. But who cares?

The bottom line is that the hole in that scarf is emblematic of a larger truth. As soon as I dreamed the image, I saw that this hole could not be repaired. There was no patch that could be put on it to hide it.

Rather it was a hole that had to be owned, seen and accepted. I realize now that the veil of my mother's infinite ability to charm me has worn through. It is my job to finally tell the truth and own what happened in my childhood.

I'm inclined to love charmers of all kinds: weavers of big tales, blue-eyed beauties, charismatic front-of-the-room types. How I want to believe their clever, seductive stories – just like I wanted to be seduced by my mother and her Grace Kelly appeal. This has gotten me into trouble more than once, for I was a girl with a big imagination and I still am. I wanted my life to play out in sunlit lace, just like a really good romance circa 1962.

And sometimes it did – for as many dark recesses as our family slid into, there were also gorgeous highs: Coming in from sledding to my mother's amazing spaghetti dinners. Trips to her best friend's house to swim and eat take-out real Philly cheesesteaks. Blissful shopping trips downtown to Bonwit Teller's to pick out the perfect outfit.

How I have feasted on these memories, playing them again and again in my mind – even as I navigated the utter chaos of life.

There's a word for this. It's called denial.

I can't remember much of the abuse my borderline mother dealt me because I was too busy hanging onto the fantasy that my childhood was "just fine."

This fantasy existed because it was necessary to protect my soul from the plate hurling, the fights, and the name-calling. I went to bed scared and woke up scared, never knowing when Mom the Monster would emerge again. I lived on the edge of my nerves throughout most of my childhood, terrified I would make a slip and do the wrong thing.

I assumed everybody lived this way.

Lately, my sister and I have been having some powerful conversations. Unlike me, she remembers exactly what happened. And why. And when. Our past helps explain why I have chosen some of the love partners I have. And why I have shrunk from my own power again and again in this life, out of nothing more than fear of reprisal.

I see now that my mother was rendered jealous by all that I had to give – except for those times she was actually proud, God bless her.

The very sad truth is that my mother really *did* give me the best she could, just as all mothers do. How could she not? We are biochemically wired to deliver warmth, food, love and shelter to our kids. Even the most severely psychotic among us must respond some way and somehow. There simply is no other choice.

Yet when there is a thin margin between your duties as a mother and your own mental illness, there is hell to pay. With that hell comes all the attendant baggage.

Now I consider the hole in Mom's scarf an omen of sorts. It's a warning to not rush myself in the healing process, nor to throw the book at my mother like a stern traffic court judge. That tattered hole is a warning to take good care of myself as I tread these rough waters, a warning to observe, record and feel, thoughtfully and thoroughly.

And to remember that despite the harshness, my mother truly loved me. She gave me that scarf one day as an act of love, even though it was one of her favorites. She wanted more than anything to avoid being the vindictive, erratic shrew that her own mother was.

Even in her pain, Boo told me how she loved me again and again, and I know it is true. Just as we all do – no matter how sad or distorted that love may get.

Now, as I own what happened, my most tender feelings are beginning to emerge. And I am sinking into the surrender that reality really is the best choice. Always.

What could I have done to prevent my mother's addiction and abuse? Nothing. And what could she have done to prevent it? Not much, given what she was dealing with and how little support she gave herself along the way.

As with everything, it was all part of God's most perfect design, delivered for me to deconstruct one day so I can share it with you. For in this writing is my own healing. If you can relate to this, perhaps yours is as well.

God bless you, Boo, wherever you are.

Slowly I am finding my way back to gratitude for all that you once were.

On Loving My Imperfection
᧰ June 26

THIS JUST IN: We are imperfect. All of us, always and forever. And here's the great news: Within that imperfection actually lies our perfection. Perhaps that is the point of this crazy rollercoaster ride we call life.

If this sounds like a koan or a word puzzle, it is – in a way. I say this as a recovering perfectionist because everyone has to find his or her way through this truth to truly get it.

What I now see in this great unfolding is how raggedly I've run myself throughout my life in the pursuit of that invisible ghost, perfection.

Last week I commented that I was doing nothing but healing right now – and doing my damnedest to say "No." As in, "No, I can't go out for tea, though I would love to" or "No, I can't show up and be anything but somewhat of a mess right now."

No, I can't be Superwoman at this exact moment in my life.

That "No" is sacred to me, and a bit strange and unfamiliar at the same time. I've begun to see my life as being divided into two phases: "Before Teal's Death" and "After Teal's Death." And within that distinction is a clear and powerful lesson.

Before my beautiful daughter's death, I was driven, relentless, a harsh taskmaster in my business and a very bossy wife. I seldom used the word "No" because I had no patience for it.

Nor did I like those who flung the word "No" back at me. I was a "Yes" girl. Proudly.

If I came up with a business idea at 3 o'clock on a Saturday afternoon, then I expected my team to be available to hash it out with me then and there – and have a sales page up by Monday evening or Tuesday at the latest. My modus operandi was "I drive myself relentlessly so you should, too." Needless to say, team members came and went with alarming frequency.

A note in Teal's journal reads: "Mom increasingly intense and grumpy before each Spiritual Marketing Quest event. I really have to speak to her about this."

That's true. I felt I personally had to pull 150 rabbits out of my hat – all by myself – forgetting, of course, that I had a fantastic business partner and a loyal, effective team to support me.

My life before Teal's death was all about me, me, me. I was driven by my secret belief that if I didn't clamp down and control every aspect of everything that things simply wouldn't get done. Or they would be done poorly.

My pain was also about my desperate attempt to hang onto my success. I believed I had to be successful at any cost; if I wasn't, the bottom was simply going to drop out.

Then, despite my efforts, the bottom did drop out and my beautiful, compassionate, soulful daughter suddenly died. Like a surreal slap in the face, something happened that no amount of doing could have prevented.

In the space of three hours I went from chatting over dinner with her in a nice restaurant to looking down at her lifeless body, comatose and in critical condition, in a hospital trauma unit.

As I stood there helplessly, I knew that this was all part of a larger plan. That no matter how much I thought, did, planned or strategized, I could not control reality. All I could do was embrace it.

I remember putting my hands on her feet – the only part of her body that was exposed. A nurse said to me kindly, "This must be so hard for you." At that moment the extent of Teal's brain damage was unclear. No one knew if Teal would die or survive in a barely functioning vegetative state for the rest of her life. Or maybe the impossible would happen and she would wake up and fully recover. The situation was truly unknowable.

"I can't fight this ... it's simply what is," I heard myself say. All of my insistent organizing of life and those around me had suddenly come to a screeching halt. "Life is change," I concluded.

"I'm so glad you understand that," the kind nurse said. She had clearly seen so many fight the inevitable when, of course, there was nothing to be done.

Since Teal's death I have slowed down to what I would call a human and humane pace.

Three months after she died, I stopped working, i.e. drumming up ways to make money that might or might not involve what my soul was calling me to do. I had taken the requisite six weeks to get my feet under me again. Then I jumped back in the fire and tried to launch a business I'd been building for many months.

My heart wasn't in it, of course. My soul wasn't either. Both actually thought I was kind of crazy – and I suppose I was. I was simply terrified to let go of my old way of being, and just "be" with my grief, my shock, my heartache.

Please God don't let me feel these harrowing feelings, I thought.

Finally, sanity and my business coach, Andrea, prevailed. "Let go," she advised, and so I did, grudgingly. I gave myself a strict two months before I intended to buckle down and get back to work.

Thankfully, I'm still in that letting-go process. January came and went. May came and went. And still I was not ready to get "back to work." In fact, I'm not sure I ever will, at least in the same way.

I've decided this is my work: writing, reflecting, being in the flow of life and seeing what my ultimate superior, God, has in mind for me on a day-to-day basis. I'm done with strategically organizing my business for maximum sales, overworking, and controlling everyone around me to make sure they jump through the appointed hoops.

In fact, after making amends to the various staffers who I left somewhat bruised, I closed that business down completely. Now I am in a period of intense listening, a process that honors my imperfection, instead of my would-be perfection. And so I relax into the great inevitability that is life, enjoying each messy moment as it comes and goes.

This grief is a place of supreme letting go, rich with possibilities. For here I have made a new and unexpected friend, happiness. I am lit from within now, and my old, blissful child-self emerges just a little more each day.

Perhaps this is something we can all take from Teal's death – the understanding that all of that striving and doing we fill our days with is just smoke in the wind. By allowing in uncertainty, we truly make our mark in the world.

Won't you join me in this beautiful, nebulous field of dreams?

A Word About Feasting on Stress
🪝 July 17

IN AMERICA, WE are addicted to stress as a nation and as individuals. It provides us with an identity and a holy reason for being, one that trumps simpler, subtler experiences like being, feeling, and noticing.

In short, if we are stressed then we are fighting "the good fight." In fact, we are only fighting ourselves.

I write this as I emerge from a lifelong immersion in stress. This was first noted by my fourth-grade teacher, Miss Brown, who wrote on my report card, "Suzanne seems worried all the time."

In fact, between my alcoholic, borderline mother and my beleaguered father, and their ongoing financial drama – about which I knew far more than any 9-year-old should, I had plenty to worry about. And then there were the school bullies who were usually nipping at my heels.

What I have come to understand is that stress is a learned condition, one which we create and consciously choose again and again and again.

Often, we don't even know we are doing it. In its own way, stress becomes habitual and even comfortable.

How do I know this? Making the decision to take the last year off was one of the most profoundly difficult things I've ever done. I told myself I shouldn't spend my savings this way, that I needed that money for my retirement.

Truthfully, I was more afraid to feel the cascades of deeper and deeper grief that were invading my body as the shock of Teal's death wore off. In fact, being immersed in my feelings was about the last place I wanted to be.

So I did what I knew: I created large amounts of stress to feast on. Namely, I tried to run my business when I could barely concentrate on anything. Then, during my time off, I angrily obsessed over my former girlfriend, who had dumped me six months prior.

Was it a good thing we broke up? Yes. Unequivocally. I can now say honestly the learning was done there and it was time for us both to move on. And I am actually much happier now without her.

But I still gnashed my teeth. And so my gut churned on and on in that old familiar rumble while my grief waited patiently in the wings for its day.

This stress I knew; it was age old. It was a perspective on life I'd taught myself as a child: Do whatever you can to try to manage this wild, out-of-control rollercoaster of a life because, baby, it's pretty much all you've got.

One day I journaled in exasperation and Spirit's guidance to me was succinct: *"Your attachment to anxiety is your attachment to your former partner, for she provides the mix of anxiety and adrenaline you need. You are feasting on stress. That's the only way to put it."*

When I asked why, I got this:

"It puts you in control in an out-of-control situation. You know what to do when you think things to death by worrying, loathing, and obsessing. That's how you stay out of your deeper feelings. By spinning your wheels you can forget how much pain you are in."

So true.

It's ironic because when we're immersed in our stress we think we're feeling our feelings. Actually, I've learned that obsessing angrily over something you can't have or fretting over a needed result is a topline emotional experience. It's like an electrical shock to your heart.

Behind it lies the real emotion, which in my case was deep, wrenching grief and a considerable amount of fear.

When I say we are addicted to stress, this is what I mean. It's like our addiction to Krispy-Kreme donuts, episodes of Downton Abbey, or shopping for shoes. We do it when we're bothered or bored.

Behind bothered or bored, there's scary stuff, like the boss, husband, or parent who humiliates and controls us – or the credit card debt that feels like it's getting out of hand ... The myriad fears, regrets, and daily woes stack up like so much firewood in our hearts, until they become the grief and the pain that we just can't admit.

These are also the very same things we assume we can't change.

But after a while, of course, everything must unravel. That is the way of Nature and of life. But instead of dealing with it head-on, we find ourselves overworking, overeating, having financial panic, or, in my case, angrily obsessing over someone who dumped me.

There just doesn't seem to be any other way to manage it.

Ah, but there is. Anti-stress programs lead us first to meditation, yoga, and counting to ten and slowing down, which is where the light of day can dawn on our feelings.

But will we go there? Will we have the courage to admit that something is wrong? That change needs to be made by us and not by anyone else?

This is where the emotional rubber meets the road. We can stop feasting on stress when we can finally admit we had a part in creating the problems that weigh us down.

In my own case, I fought like hell the sad fact that my

partner was not in love with me. I knew it months before she told me, but my weeping heart could not admit it. Even more so, the truth I really ran from was that I was not in love with her.

I loved the concept of "us," the frisson of having a fun, beautiful woman on my arm. And I loved the way we could laugh together. But at the end of the day ours was a loving friendship that we kept trying to force into a box labeled "Love."

Was this the deep intimate relationship I longed for? No, despite all the twists of my imagination that refused to see the truth, it simply was what it was, for better or for worse. In my acceptance of this truth, just as in my acceptance of Teal's early death, I have found release.

At the end of the day we have only one choice. To see, own, and embrace what is.

The end of all stress means having the courage to honor our feelings as sacred channels of the truth and listening to our bodies as keepers of that infinite wisdom.

Herein lies all that is good and whole in life. And so it is.

Emptying Teal's Closet:
A Study in Fun, Love and Polka Dots
❦ July 29

OVER THE WEEKEND I did something I haven't had the strength to do until now: I cleaned out Teal's closet.

Her closet was like my purse, a receptacle for all that truly matters. Teal did not drive a car, nor did she even drive her own life. Instead, her existence was a study in being, most of it directed toward fun.

Fun was catalogued in the offbeat "experimental" items – yellow polka-dotted sneakers for instance – and clothing written on by friends. "Teal + Sophie + Luke" and "Be Free!"

It was all there despite the fact that one month prior to her death, she had gone through her things and thrown out a lot. As if she wanted to leave a well-0rganized legacy.

In fact, Teal left behind a record for how we all might approach life. And so I do my best, between sobs, to record what I learned in this closet-based journey through her days.

She kept things for the sweet memories they evoked: cheap, clingy T-shirts with wistful designs, reminiscent of high school Saturdays at the mall; her white polyester gown from her high school graduation; prom gowns secured in dry cleaning bags.

I also found a random smattering of truly odd items: neon orange fishnets, a hot pink mini-kilt, and a white wool bustier with a strangely collegiate blue cable knitted into it.

That was Teal. She always made a point of dressing outside the box, combining plaids and prints with anything else she could think of, a practice that began as a toddler. Clothing was an all-dessert buffet to my girl, and she delighted in the exploration of every flavor.

One day, when Teal was four, she announced she would wear her favorite pink pleated skirt and her Mary Janes to school. And nothing else. Teal was not messing around when it came to fun, no siree.

Deep in her core, she also believed in the energy of all things, which, I suspect, is why I found the small pair of lavender cotton pajamas printed with stars I bought for her when she was eight years old. Along with the hot pink shirt covered with iridescent ladybugs, her favorite item at age six.

Teal had invested too much love in these items to throw them away.

And then there were her beautiful floral sundresses. They were so imbued with summer, with picking strawberries, with hours and hours with nothing to do but laze in the grass, with all of the hope and possibility that life at its carefree best invokes.

T-shirts chronicled life events: volunteering in Africa ("Ghana @ 50"), an appearance in the musical Cabaret ("Life is Wonderful!"), her trip to Morocco with her dad when she was ten, and her job as a hostess at The Old Dock.

And there were several pairs of Keds worn nearly through from backpacking her way around the world. Sneakers she wore well past their prime because life was to be explored fully, wasn't it?

As I dug deeper into her closet, layers fell away, revealing more and more about what was of greatest importance to Teal.

A tangled ball of hand wraps from her beloved San Francisco gym where she practiced Thai Boxing and learned about her own mettle emerged. And there was the stack of childhood scripts from the theater where she learned to perform beginning at age six – 17 shows in all.

I also found her warm-up jacket from high school soccer, her name stitched on the sleeve. Teal was no athlete, but how she loved being part of something bigger than herself. The glue of a team of girls trying their best on the playing fields of an Adirondack autumn was its own aphrodisiac.

And I found her beloved blue T-shirt, shot through with holes, the words "Peace Corps" nearly invisible on it. It was purchased by her father, a retired Peace Corps volunteer, years before she was born. He'd gotten it for the child he hoped he might have someday.

Teal wore it to tatters in high school and to her admissions interview at Berklee. That day she sat in the waiting room filled with hopeful musicians in their suits and dresses. By contrast, Teal was proud and confident in her ratty Peace Corps T-shirt, ready to save the world with her music and her message. It was one of the great wins of her life when she got in.

Finally, behind everything, I found something in Teal's closet that brought me to my knees.

I'd been working along steadily as I sorted and folded. This is going so well, I thought to myself. But when I found this one thing I had to finally lie down on the floor and surrender to my grief.

Here was the hand-painted, six-foot-long banner her father had stayed up all night making on the night she was born. "Welcome Home Teal!" it announced proudly in carefully painted letters. On it were the signatures of every person who came to visit her in those first precious weeks.

Every inch of it is filled with the deep love and promise of our marriage – the coming together of two souls who may not have always agreed and in the end were no longer compatible. Yet we knew enough to fulfill our souls' purposes together, and so Teal and her brother Luke were born.

Lovingly, hour after hour, I folded each of Teal's items into paper bags from Trader Joes that said, "Please Recycle This Bag." All of it would go to Goodwill, which is just what she would have wanted.

As I worked and wept, and then fell apart completely, I began to accept the impossible. My little girl really is gone but she is also right here, alive within me and as full of love as ever. This is true for all of us, both the quick and the dead.

I left what should be left in her closet – a dozen items representing each stage of her life, including that glorious sign, folded neatly and displayed on a shelf – along with plenty of empty space for what must emerge next.

We should never hang on to what has departed but let it go in full gratitude and grace, knowing that what has come to be is always for the best. No matter how sudden. No matter how dramatic. And no matter how painful.

You truly are in a better place, Teal. I know that much after celebrating your life, hanger by hanger, piece by piece. And curiously, happily, I am in a better place now as well.

Perhaps this was just what you had in mind.

My Declaration of Independence
🔊 August 14

AND THERE CAME a time when I had to finally emerge, to release my mother, my story, my struggle and my suffering. I had to release my grip on so-called reality. By that, I mean I had to let go of the steely, inflexible view with which I have seen myself most of my life – a "reality" that was witheringly harsh. It led me to angry, controlling lovers, compulsive behaviors, and smaller work in which I could hide for years and years.

In doing so, I crafted a reality that wasn't actually real.

If I don't let go of this, no business can be built, no writing can be truly shared, and no destiny can be lived. I cannot make the impact I was born to make. This place of illusion feels safe and comfortable. Yet it is also a place of stasis.

Here is what I'm learning about coming into my own in this, my fifty-fourth year: *It is safe to be seen and heard.* I no longer have to hide in any way – spiritual, emotional, strategic or otherwise.

I no longer have to sequester myself in inappropriate work that is a cover for my greatness. And I don't have to be a "success story" that's really about scoring validation and avoiding the thing I was born to do.

Now I really know the truth: I was born to move people by writing and speaking from the heart.

So why would a perfectly decent writer and speaker hide from her much-loved crafts? Many reasons. As a child it was about protecting my mother from the sense that she, herself, was a failure by comparison.

Oh, how my mother struggled with her own anxiety and insecurity. Nothing was ever good enough. Ever. So many dreams got laid to dust, incomplete. She became a woman who lived solely for her children. And I, a sensitive child, didn't want to forge ahead and surpass her.

It just didn't seem like good form.

Then there was always the sheer terror of truly emerging. For what I know now is that this writing is only meant to exist in one form: fantastically honest – without a shred of pretense.

It doesn't require particular effort. Nor does it need much more time and space. What it demands is simple courage.

I can no longer be the guarded, wary person I once was to do this work. I must be that essential self – what my former husband called my "little flower." He knew it was in there, just as others have. But how frightened I have always been of this flower, this self, this Suzanne.

But, now, the flower is opening. The writing has begun. And it is unstoppable. And so I show up to feed this beautiful engine that has patiently waited for me all these years. The feeding of it is the feeding of me – a Me I can now proudly reclaim.

Three things happened in the past few days that confirm this transition has begun.

First, I woke up to find a bat flying around the room I've been sleeping in, Teal's childhood bedroom. Where the bat came from is a mystery, but there it was, big and black and coming right at me.

According to a shamanic website, the bat is a harbinger of a new beginning and the release of the old, which is precisely what I'd determined this particular trip East would be for me. It marks a turning point, a shift in my grief as we near the one-year anniversary of Teal's death.

Then last night I had a dream in which I was back at The New York Times, where I once worked in the marketing department. In the dream, I was trying to sneak into a meeting for the editorial writers. They said, "Suzanne, why aren't you taking your seat here in the front? This is for you and your writing."

I'd been discovered! How afraid I felt. I was so resistant to God's very gift for me. I had to get back to the marketing department – they'd be looking for me! Yet here was the recognition I'd always craved but never sought to claim, even when I actually worked at the Times.

Perhaps I wasn't ready then. I had to live more, lose more, and surrender so much more. Instead of being more "mighty" I had to become more undone before I could finally claim that one precious pearl I had left, my own sweet soul.

That brings me to the third incident, a brief snippet of a dream in which a jaguar embraced me. As I wrapped my arms around its massive cat shoulders and nuzzled my face into its warm, golden neck, I heard its forceful purring. And I knew it loved me. As did the huge, aging, slightly beaten-up dog that joined us. This dog was my inner protector, just as the jaguar was my power. I knew I loved them both immeasurably.

So I step forth, gently and carefully, minding my way and feeding myself just what I need as I go. This is the only way we can ever honor the God-self that we are. By listening, understanding, and providing ourselves with exactly what we need.

Today, I have awakened to this new, beautiful reality with Teal riding shotgun on my shoulder. And if I die before I wake, I pray the Lord my soul to take, through pieces of my writing, scattered throughout the Universe like stars. Or slices of the very best chocolate cake.

What I know now is my soul is yours for the taking, for I am no longer afraid.

August 21

TODAY MARKS THE first anniversary of Teal's death. In remembrance of her, I share her "Full Moon Prayer," written seven weeks before she died. I found it on a small scrap of notebook paper among her belongings.

"Love for all the enemies who have fought and can't agree. A time of resolution or at least compromise. A time for transformation of the body, mind and soul. Transformation of the heart to transcend any thoughts that could

bring it down to the level of pettiness and greed. I pray for peace among my family and friends. May we all rest well together. And finally, I pray that we all obtain clarity of our existence and what is. (Myself included!) Thank you Moon gods and goddesses. Love, Teal."

A Real and Lasting Happiness
๛ September 18

IT BEGAN QUIETLY. ⸴

Day by day. Week by week. Month by month, joy began to seep in.

A true living, breathing, practical happiness became mine, just when I least expected it.

Over time, I have begun to worry less and take life more lightly. Notably absent are a husband – or a wife – and my children, although my beautiful son Luke does pop in occasionally. It's usually by email with something hilarious to share or perhaps a technical request about things like laundry, grammar, or college expenses.

Also absent are the big house, the driving business, the big, dazzling accomplishments and the schedule jam-packed with "critical" tasks. Gone are the usual markers I always held up as "success," which is when I assumed I'd finally be happy.

So why this beautiful, tender, ethereal joy? Why now and why me, God?

Is it because I have been meditating, dutifully, every morning for more than a year now? Or because of California's predictably sunny weather? Or because of the easy sweet peace and humor I enjoy with my housemates Bobbie and Jeewon?

Or is it because I have come to know God in my heart and soul – as a living, breathing part of myself – so that my soul no longer feels like a refugee trudging through life?

I cannot completely explain it. But I can say I have done my work. The entire last year has been a study in surrender, from which I learned to tell the truth about my life, ask for help and get it.

But then this was what I decided when Teal died: the rest of my life would be dedicated to her memory. To living the life she could not, with power, grace, authenticity, and, most of all, with love and service to others.

And so in this way Teal, who wanted with all her heart to be a healer, has healed her mother.

I can now make peace where I once made messes. I feel a new, tender grace about things that once bothered me. For instance, I stopped thinking about my former girlfriend as some pariah sent down to hurt me. My need to vilify her is gone and I now regard her with compassion and true empathy – as I do anyone who has hurt me in my life.

This compassion-empathy bit is new. My housemate Bobbie and I talked about this last night.

"But haven't you always felt compassion for others?" she asked.

"No," I answered evenly, making both of us laugh.

My compassion was always furtive – darting in, hopefully unseen –because if you caught me in that pants-around-my-ankles moment, I might be exposed. It made me feel too vulnerable, too weak.

The truth is I can be more compassionate with others because I have learned to be compassionate with myself, and not just through massages and ice cream sundaes. Now I comfort myself in the middle of the night, when worry collides with reason and my imagination runs wild. Then I slowly tether my galloping thoughts and ease them back into their corrals.

I find myself setting healthy boundaries that I couldn't set before, and saying "No" with love and kindness. Mostly, I reassure myself that God's got my back and that I have nothing to fear. And so I can naturally relax.

Ironically, this renders me so much more powerful than before.

So I move through life with a new, delicate strength, just feeling my way along, one step at a time. And I see myself emerging as I edit these essays into a book for publication and prepare to give talks for anyone who will listen.

This is the life I promised Teal when she was dying.

One of the last afternoons of her life, when she lay motionless in a coma, my friends Rick and Brian came to visit Teal. And she gave Rick a telepathic message. "This is my stage," he clearly heard her say.

And so it is.

Teal's natural love and compassion for the world – her greatest natural gift – has become mine to share. But only through my complete surrender to a whole new way of being, informed by love and honesty.

This happiness feels so new. And hopeful. And beautiful. And it has that holy rightness we know at birth, that precious sense that somehow slips away over time. Yet you are a child of God, as am I, and so this peace is here for every last one of us.

This Joy is free for the taking, dear friend. All you have to be is brave – and decide, like I have, that you deserve it.

If nothing else, that was Teal's dearest wish for us all.

Want an extra boost of self care? Get Suzanne's free Loving Self Care Bundle...all yours in a click at suzannefalter.com/self-care

You can find Suzanne on Facebook at www.facebook.com/svfalter

Her other books, products and programs, and speaking calendar, can be found at www.suzannefalter.com

Finally, would you consider leaving a review of Surrendering to Joy *on Amazon? We would be highly grateful! Thank you for your consideration.*

About the Author

Suzanne Falter is an author, speaker and blogger who tells 'fearless stories' – highly vulnerable essays about grief and joy, novels about uncommon heroes who overcome the odds, and a memoir about finding her way back after the sudden death of her daughter Teal. Her online writing and videos can be found on Facebook, Twitter, YouTube and Pinterest. You can find her 'Fearless Stories' ezine at www.suzannefalter.com.

Additional Non-Fiction by Suzanne Falter
How Much Joy Can You Stand?
Living Your Joy

Fiction by Suzanne Falter & Jack Harvey
Transformed: San Francisco
Transformed: Paris

Acknowledgements

I WISH TO express my gratitude to the many readers of my Face-book profile page, where these essays first appeared in the year following Teal's death. Their love, support, and nakedly honest shares helped carry me through my grief. I wish to especially thank my "Surrender to Joy Friends," whose loving, thoughtful feedback guided the production of this book.

I also wish to thank my mentor and dear friend, Andrea J. Lee, for her ongoing support of my professional work, as well as Elizabeth Marshall for her sage publishing advice.

—SVF

Made in the USA
San Bernardino, CA
22 August 2017